Junior Teach Yourself Books

EDITED BY LEONARD CUTTS

COOKERY

Junior Teach Yourself Books

A Junior Teach Yourself Book

COOKERY

BY

MARGARET G. LASKIE

Lecturer in Domestic Science Methods,
Jordanhill Training College

THE ENGLISH UNIVERSITIES PRESS LTD

102, NEWGATE STREET, LONDON, E.C.1.

PRINTED IN ENGLAND
FOR THE ENGLISH UNIVERSITIES PRESS, LTD.,
BY ELLIOTT BROS. AND YEOMAN, LTD., LIVERPOOL,
AND BOUND BY C. TINLING AND CO., LTD., LIVERPOOL, LONDON AND PRESCOT.

Introduction

HAVE you ever said, "I love when Mother lets me try making something for tea, but Mother's cookery book doesn't always explain just what to do?"

Yes, and in the end you have to ask Mother to come and help you out of your difficulty.

The recipe said, ' When the mixture is of the correct consistency, pour the mixture into prepared tin and bake in a moderate oven.'

You have the mixture ready but the recipe did not say how to prepare the tin, nor that the tin should have been prepared before you began measuring the ingredients, nor that the oven should have been heated first of all!

Grown-ups take so much for granted!

Well, here is the very book for you—written in simple language which you will understand and if you read through the recipes very carefully you will notice that the method of making is planned to make it easier for you and that many small difficulties are explained.

Here, too, you will find that I have tried to help you by sketching some of the processes and suggesting suitable utensils and pans to use.

Start studying the sketches at the top left-hand corner and trace each step till you arrive at the finished dish, so now, make your choice and go ahead!

Remember that not only should food be well-cooked but that it must also look attractive and be served very daintily, and if you carry out these three points of advice you will be well on the way to being a successful cook—and a well-cooked meal makes a difference to happiness and contentment in the home.

May this little book give you as much pleasure and enjoyment as it gave me to make it—specially for you!

Contents

WHAT YOU MUST REMEMBER

Attend to
fire, heat oven.
Collect all utensils and
ingredients beforehand.
Read recipes carefully and
measure accurately.
Begin with the dishes requiring
longest cooking.
Attend to pans or oven while
cooking is in progress.
Avoid wasting fuel. Do not have
the gas coming up the sides of pan.
Turn off heat when cooking is finished.
Do not use larger pans than necessary.
Use flat-bottomed pans with an electric
cooker for contact.
Keep an eye on the clock.
Clear away and wash up as you go along.
Taste before serving.
Serve quickly and neatly. Serve punctually.

CARE OF THE KITCHEN
" A place for everything and everything in its place."

1. Start the day's work in good time.
2. Clean up as you go along.
3. Check up all foodstuffs, etc., when received.
4. Keep invoices and all receipts in a file.
5. After dinner, wash dishes and give kitchen a daily clean, i.e. sweep and dust.
   Tidy up.

KITCHEN CUPBOARD FOR
KEEPING CEREALS, e.g.
FLOUR, SUGAR, MEAL, etc.

LARDER FOR KEEPING MILK,
BUTTER, CHEESE, etc.

VEGETABLE RACK

WASHING OF DISHES, ETC.

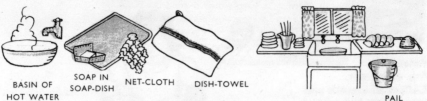

BASIN OF HOT WATER   SOAP IN SOAP-DISH   NET-CLOTH   DISH-TOWEL   PAIL FOR SCRAPS

METHOD

1. Put leftover food on clean saucers in larder.
2. Collect dishes, cutlery, etc. Put scraps in brock-pail.
3. Rub greasy dishes first with paper. Have dishes piled neatly together at one side of sink.
4. Steep cutlery, handles out, in jug of water. Empty tea-leaves into paper and burn.
5. Rinse milk jugs in cold water.
6. Place tray for draining dishes at other side of sink.
7. Fill basin with hot water and make soapy lather with cake of soap. Do not leave soap in water.
8. Have ready a net-cloth for washing and a dish-towel for drying.
9. Begin by washing glass (see that water is not too hot, as glass cracks easily). Dry.
10. Wash cutlery, taking care to remove food from prongs of forks. Dry, rubbing well. Place on tray or in cutlery box.
11. Wash cleanest dishes first. A lump of washing soda can be added to water for washing greasy dishes, but never use soda if dishes have colour or gilt.
12. Drain upside down, resting plates carefully on a bowl—or use draining-rack.
13. When dishes are quite dry, put away in cupboard.
14. Wash and dry soap-dish, basin, etc. Scrub wood round sink, rinse and dry (page 9).
15. Clean sink with suitable cleanser.
16. Place a lump of soda over grating and pour down some boiling water to leave trap clean.
17. Wash out net-cloth and dish-towel in hot soapy water, rinse in hot water, then cold. Wring and hang up.
18. Empty waste food into pig-bin at end of each day and wash well. Disinfect once a week.

Note.—If pans have also to be washed in same sink, do not clean sink till all work is done.

WASHING OF PANS, LIDS & TINS

METHOD

1. **Steep pans** as soon as they are emptied-starchy pans in cold water. Burnt pans-fill with cold water, add a lump of washing soda and bring slowly to the boil. Leave to steep several hours.
2. For washing, collect pot-brush or wire pot cleaner, pan mixture and a small cloth for applying.
3. For drying have a coarse brown towel.
4. Fill sink with hot water and make soapy lather with hard soap.
5. Place wooden pot-board in sink to protect surface of sink.
6. Wash pans thoroughly, inside and out, using cleanser if necessary.
7. Add a lump of soda to water for very greasy pans, but do not use for aluminium. Polish up aluminium pans with wire pot cleaner or steel wool.
8. Dry with brown cloth and place near warmth to dry off.
9. **Pan lids** are washed in same way as pans. Polish tops with plate powder. Rub up with duster.
   Tins. Scour with pan mixture, cleanser or steel wool. Rinse and dry with brown cloth. Dry off in warmth.
10. Rinse pot-brush, etc. Hang up.
11. Scrub wood and dry (page 9).
12. Wash cloths in hot water, rinse, wring and dry off.
13. Clean out sink as above.

CARE OF WHITE WOOD

SCRUBBING-BRUSH

FLANNEL

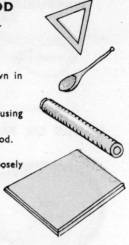

Aim. To keep wood in good condition.
To keep as white as possible.

METHOD.

1. Gather together wooden utensils.
2. Collect articles for scrubbing, as shown in illustration.
3. Half fill zinc bath with warm water.
4. Wash over wood with warm water, using a flannel, loosely wrung out.
5. Scrub the way of the grain in the wood. Be very sparing with the soap.
6. Mop up soapy water with flannel, loosely wrung out.
7. Twist flannel tightly and dry wood.
8. Place near an open window to air.
9. Put away when quite dry.

POLISHING OF CUTLERY

Cutlery should be polished once a week at home.
Stainless knives do not require polishing.
Remove polish carefully, especially from prongs of forks.

SPOONS AND FORKS

1. Collect articles.
2. Damp the small cloth and rub on plate powder. Allow to dry.
3. Rub with newspaper.
4. Shine with duster and lay on tray.
5. Tidy tin, etc., into box and wash cloths.

KNIVES AND STEEL FORKS

1. Collect articles together.
2. Scrape bathbrick into saucer and rub on blades with small damp cloth.
3. Rub with newspaper.
4. Shine with duster and lay on tray.
5. Tidy box and wash cloths.

HANDY MEASURES

CEREALS

POWDERS e.g., FLOUR CORNFLOUR, CUSTARD POWDER, etc.

I rounded tablespoon weighs I oz.   I rounded dessertspoon weighs $\frac{1}{2}$ oz.   I rounded teaspoon weighs $\frac{1}{4}$ oz.

OTHER GRAINS, e.g., SUGAR, SEMOLINA, RICE, etc.

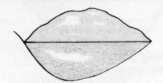

I level tablespoon weighs I oz.   I level dessertspoon weighs $\frac{1}{2}$ oz.   I level teaspoon weighs $\frac{1}{4}$ oz.

MEASURING BAKING SODA, CREAM OF TARTAR, BAKING POWDER, SALT, etc.

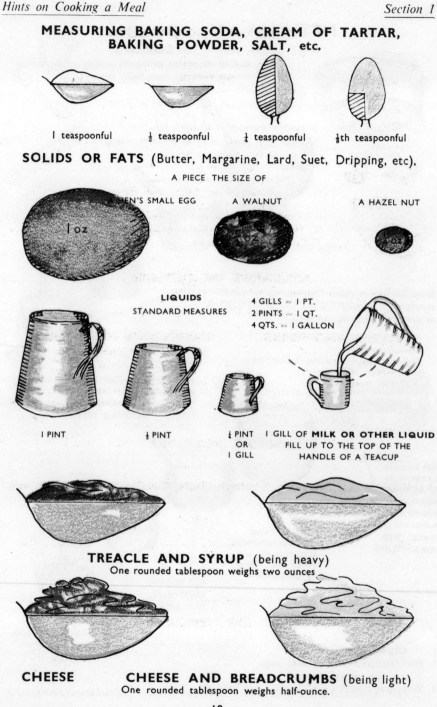

I teaspoonful   ½ teaspoonful   ¼ teaspoonful   ⅛th teaspoonful

SOLIDS OR FATS (Butter, Margarine, Lard, Suet, Dripping, etc).

A PIECE THE SIZE OF

HEN'S SMALL EGG   A WALNUT   A HAZEL NUT

1 oz   1 oz   ½ oz

LIQUIDS
STANDARD MEASURES

4 GILLS = 1 PT.
2 PINTS = 1 QT.
4 QTS. = 1 GALLON

1 PINT   ½ PINT   ¼ PINT   1 GILL OF **MILK OR OTHER LIQUID**
OR   FILL UP TO THE TOP OF THE
1 GILL   HANDLE OF A TEACUP

TREACLE AND SYRUP (being heavy)
One rounded tablespoon weighs two ounces

CHEESE   CHEESE AND BREADCRUMBS (being light)
One rounded tablespoon weighs half-ounce.

METHODS OF COOKING.
BOILING.

Boiling is cooking in rapidly boiling water, having enough water to completely cover.

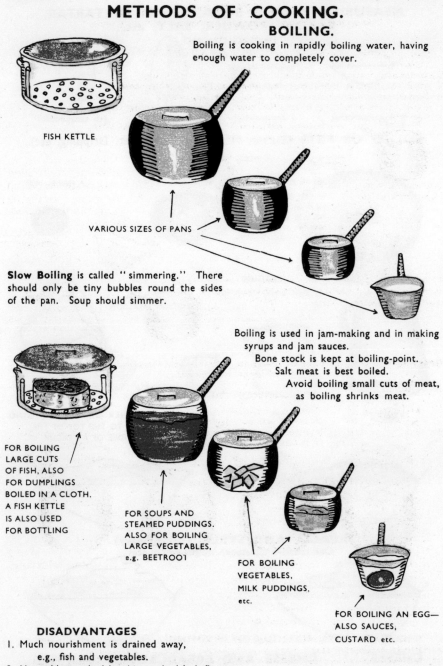

FISH KETTLE

VARIOUS SIZES OF PANS

Slow Boiling is called "simmering." There should only be tiny bubbles round the sides of the pan. Soup should simmer.

Boiling is used in jam-making and in making syrups and jam sauces.
Bone stock is kept at boiling-point.
Salt meat is best boiled.
Avoid boiling small cuts of meat, as boiling shrinks meat.

FOR BOILING LARGE CUTS OF FISH, ALSO FOR DUMPLINGS BOILED IN A CLOTH. A FISH KETTLE IS ALSO USED FOR BOTTLING

FOR SOUPS AND STEAMED PUDDINGS. ALSO FOR BOILING LARGE VEGETABLES, e.g. BEETROOT

FOR BOILING VEGETABLES, MILK PUDDINGS, etc.

FOR BOILING AN EGG— ALSO SAUCES, CUSTARD etc.

DISADVANTAGES
1. Much nourishment is drained away, e.g., fish and vegetables.
2. Vegetables cooked by this method lack flavour.

11

STEAMING

Steaming is cooking in the vapour produced by boiling liquid.

INSTRUCTIONS

1. Bowl should be a size smaller than pan for ease in lifting out. Grease bowl and paper to cover.
2. Bowl should be only two-thirds full of mixture to allow for rising.
3. Have enough water in pan to come half-way up the sides of the bowl.
4. Keep water boiling and have a kettle of boiling water ready to fill up as required.
5. Allow a steamed pudding to stand for a few minutes before turning out.

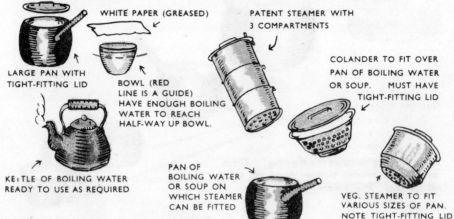

LARGE PAN WITH TIGHT-FITTING LID

WHITE PAPER (GREASED)

BOWL (RED LINE IS A GUIDE) HAVE ENOUGH BOILING WATER TO REACH HALF-WAY UP BOWL.

PATENT STEAMER WITH 3 COMPARTMENTS

COLANDER TO FIT OVER PAN OF BOILING WATER OR SOUP. MUST HAVE TIGHT-FITTING LID

KETTLE OF BOILING WATER READY TO USE AS REQUIRED

PAN OF BOILING WATER OR SOUP ON WHICH STEAMER CAN BE FITTED

VEG. STEAMER TO FIT VARIOUS SIZES OF PAN. NOTE TIGHT-FITTING LID

Steaming is suitable for cooking fish, meat, vegetables, puddings and delicate mixtures. It takes longer than boiling.

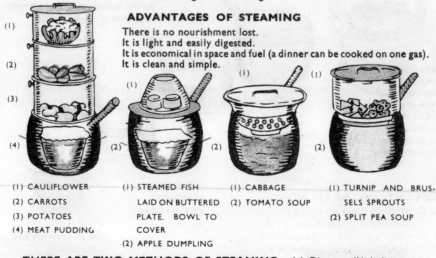

ADVANTAGES OF STEAMING

There is no nourishment lost.
It is light and easily digested.
It is economical in space and fuel (a dinner can be cooked on one gas).
It is clean and simple.

(1) CAULIFLOWER
(2) CARROTS
(3) POTATOES
(4) MEAT PUDDING

(1) STEAMED FISH LAID ON BUTTERED PLATE. BOWL TO COVER
(2) APPLE DUMPLING

(1) CABBAGE
(2) TOMATO SOUP

(1) TURNIP AND BRUSSELS SPROUTS
(2) SPLIT PEA SOUP

THERE ARE TWO METHODS OF STEAMING. (a) Direct. (b) Indirect.

(a) **Direct**—where the steam comes in contact with the food, as in vegetables.
(b) **Indirect**—where the steam comes in contact with the bowl or plate containing the food—in steaming fish, meat and puddings.

12

STEWING

Stewing is a long, slow method of cooking in an enclosed vessel, using very little liquid. It is suitable for cooking fish, meat, vegetables and fruit (fresh and dry). Aim is to render tender and to conserve the goodness.

(A)

(B)

A STEW SHOULD SIMMER,
i.e. IT SHOULD BOIL VERY GENTLY

(C)

(D)

INSTRUCTIONS

1. Choose a shallow pan with a tight-fitting lid or for oven use, a casserole or Pyrex dish.
2. Have enough liquid to cover the bottom of pan, etc.
3. If stewing meat, boil for five minutes, then simmer till food is tender.

(a) Shallow stewpan with tight-fitting lid.
(b) Fireproof casserole.
(c) Pyrex.
(d) Jam-jar with saucer to cover.

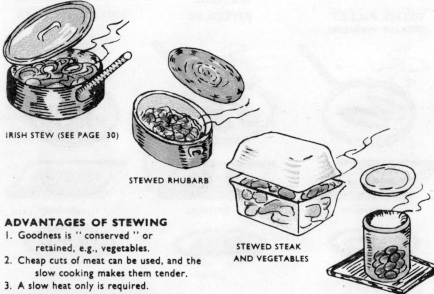

IRISH STEW (SEE PAGE 30)

STEWED RHUBARB

STEWED STEAK
AND VEGETABLES

STEWED
PRUNES

ADVANTAGES OF STEWING

1. Goodness is " conserved " or retained, e.g., vegetables.
2. Cheap cuts of meat can be used, and the slow cooking makes them tender.
3. A slow heat only is required.
4. It is a clean and simple method.

DISADVANTAGE

It is a slow method of cooking.

SHALLOW FRYING

Shallow Frying is cooking in smoking-hot fat.

Aim. (1) To prevent escape of juices and to prevent entrance of fat.

(2) To serve crisp, well-cooked and golden-brown.

INSTRUCTIONS

1. Have enough fat to come half-way up food to be fried.
2. Have fat faintly smoking.
3. Have food coated where there is no natural coating.
4. Do not put in too many articles at one time.
5. Reheat fat in between batches of frying.
6. Drain on tin with paper to absorb grease. Keep tin hot.
7. Serve immediately on hot ashet with dish-paper.

FISH-SLICE

HOT ASHET WITH DISH-PAPER

FRYING-PAN

TIN WITH PAPER TO ABSORB GREASE

FRIED FILLET
(Filleted Haddock)

FRYING RISSOLES

POTATO CHIPS

DRAINED   DRAINED   DRAINED

SERVED   SERVED   SERVED

ADVANTAGES OF SHALLOW FRYING
1. It is tasty.
2. It is a quick method.

DISADVANTAGES
1. Too much fried food is indigestible.
2. Frying is a " splashy " method of cooking.

DEEP FRYING

Frying in smoking-hot fat, having enough fat to cover food to be fried.

Aim. (1) To prevent escape of juices and to prevent entrance of fat. (2) to serve crisp, well-cooked and golden-brown.

INSTRUCTIONS

1. Use strong, deep, unlined stewpan. Melt 2 lbs. fat (dripping, suet or lard) until smoking-hot. Heat basket in fat.
2. Heat serving dish.
3. Prepare food to be fried, and coat if there is no natural coating.
4. Have food as dry as possible, e.g., potatoes—dry in clean towel.
5. When articles to be fried are coated with batter, do not use basket. Lift out with draining-spoon.
6. Do not put in too many articles at one time.
7. Reheat fat in between batches of frying.
8. Drain on paper as shown.
9. Serve immediately.

FRYING BASKET

TIN WITH PAPER FOR DRAINING

DRAINING-SPOON FOR TURNING FRIED FOOD IN PAN AND FOR LIFTING OUT WHEN BASKET IS NOT IN USE

DISH-PAPER

STRONG IRON PAN WITHOUT A LINING. HAVE ENOUGH FAT TO COVER FOOD

ASHET

LIFTED OUT WITH DRAINING-SPOON

(1)

FRIED DOUGHNUTS BASKET IS NOT USED WITH BATTER

(2)

(3)

FRIED FISH CAKES (1) BASKET HEATED IN PAN.

DRAINED ON TIN WITH PAPER

(2)

FAT SMOKING-HOT

(3)

ADVANTAGES
1. It is quick.
2. It is tasty.

DRAINED ON TIN WITH PAPER

DISADVANTAGES
1. It is indigestible.
2. It is dangerous unless great care is taken to prevent fire.

15

GRILLING

Grilling is cooking by direct rays of heat.
Aim is to make tender and to keep in the juices.
Grilling is suitable for meat, fish, bacon, sausages,
    tomatoes, lambs' and sheep's kidneys.
Meat used must be of the best quality—
Fillet steak, Pope's-eye steak.
Mutton—single or double loin chops.

FOR USE OVER
AN OPEN FIRE

GRILL   GRILL-PAN

TRIVET TO FIT GRILL-PAN

FRONT VIEW   SET OF SKEWERS

INSTRUCTIONS

1. Heat grill till red-hot; if using an open fire, have it clear and red.
2. Place kettle or pan over grill to send the heat down.
3. Heat and grease bars of grill-pan. Brush meat with melted butter.
4. Cook meat quickly on one side, then turn. Do not cut off fat beforehand.
5. Turn meat frequently with spoon and knife.
6. Time for cooking—10—12—15 minutes. Do not overcook.
7. Serve immediately on a hot ashet.

GRILLED CHOP

GRILLED KIPPER

GRILLED TOMATOES

HAVE GRILL RED HOT.
KETTLE ON TOP

GRILLED BACON

GRILLED KIDNEY AND SAUSAGE

ROASTING

Roasting is cooking in hot air radiated from the sides of the oven. It is suitable for meat.
Aim to make tender and to keep in juices.

OVEN CLOTH

INSTRUCTIONS

1. Use only best cuts of meat for roasting.
2. Arrange position of shelves beforehand.
3. Have a strong heat in oven to start the cooking.
4. Baste occasionally with smoking-hot fat to seal up the nourishment.

FAT

16

OVEN TEMPERATURES.

DIRECTIONS.

Gas Oven.

1. Light gas oven 15 minutes before using.
2. Leave door slightly open for 3 minutes.
3. Arrange shelves as desired.
4. Close oven door and set Regulo at 6 or F.
5. Change Regulo to temperature at which dish is being cooked 5 minutes before putting dish into oven.

Electricity.

1. Switch on electricity 15 minutes before putting dish into oven.
2. Allow oven door to remain open for a few minutes after switching on electricity.
3. Do not allow thermometer to rise above temperature required.

Note.—In different districts oven heat may vary so lower or raise heat accordingly.

Fish Dishes, e.g. Baked Fish, etc.
          Gas Oven: Regulo 6 or F.   Electric Oven: 350°F.

Meat Dishes other than joints and pies covered with pastry, e.g. Shepherd's Pie.
          Gas Oven: Regulo 7 or G.   Electric Oven: 375°F.

Joints, e.g. Roast Beef.
          Gas Oven: Regulo 8 or H for 5 minutes then lower to 6 or F.
          Electric Oven: 425°F for 5 minutes, lower to 375°F.

Vegetable Dishes, e.g. Potatoes, onions, tomatoes, etc.
          Gas Oven: Regulo 6 or F.   Electric Oven: 350°F.

Pastry, e.g. *Short Crust.*
          Gas Oven: Regulo 9 or I.   Electric Oven: 450°F.

          Rough Puff (for small dishes, e.g. tarts, etc.).
          Gas Oven: Regulo 9 or I, reduce to 8 or H after 5 minutes.
          Electric Oven: 450°F, reduce to 400°F after 5 minutes.

          Rough Puff (for large dishes, e.g. meat pies, etc.).
          Gas Oven: 9 or I, reduce after 10 minutes to Regulo 7 or G.
          Electric Oven: 450°F, reduce after 5 minutes to 400°F.

          Flaky Pastry (small dishes, etc.).
          Gas Oven: Regulo 9 or I, reduce to 7 or G after 5 minutes.
          Electric Oven: 500°F, reduce to 400°F after 5 minutes.

          Flaky Pastry (large dishes, e.g., pies, etc.).
          Gas Oven: Regulo 9 or I, reduce to 7 or G after 5 minutes.
          Electric Oven: 500°F, reduce to 400°F after 10 minutes.

Puddings (1) Milk (e.g. Rice).
          Gas Oven: Regulo 4 or D.   Electric Oven: 300°F.

        (2) Bread Mixtures (e.g. Bread and Butter Pudding, Queen of Puddings)
          Gas Oven: Regulo 5 or E.   Electric Oven: 350°F.

Custards (e.g. fish custard).
    Gas Oven: Regulo 5 or E. Electric Oven: 350°F.

Fruit (e.g. baked apple).
    Gas Oven: Regulo 5 or E. Electric Oven: 350°F.

Batters (e.g. Toad-in-a-Hole).
    Gas Oven: Regulo 7 or G. Electric Oven: 400°F.

"Rubbing-in" Mixtures. Small baking (e.g. scones, rock cakes, etc.).
    Gas Oven: Regulo 9 or I. Electric Oven: 450°F.

Large Cakes (e.g. Plain Fruit Cake and puddings; e.g. Eve's Pudding).
    Gas Oven: Regulo 8 or H, reduce to 7 or G after 10 minutes.
    Electric Oven: 400°F, reduce to 325°F after 10 minutes.

Biscuits (e.g. Oatmeal).
    Gas Oven: Regulo 5 or E. Electric Oven: 350°F.

"Creaming" Mixtures (Small Cakes, e.g. Queen Cakes).
    Gas Oven: Regulo 9 or I. Electric Oven: 450°F.

Large Cakes (e.g. White Cake).
    Gas Oven: Regulo 7 or G for 15 minutes, reduce to 5 or E for remainder of time.
    Electric Oven: 400°F, reduce to 350°F after 10 to 15 minutes.

Puddings (e.g. Eve's Pudding).
    Gas Oven: Regulo 8 or H, reduce after 10 minutes to 7 or G.
    Electric Oven: 450°F, reduce after 10 minutes to 400°F.

Biscuits (e.g. Shortbread, Empire biscuits).
    Gas Oven: Regulo 5 or E. Electric Oven: 300°F.

Sponge Mixtures, e.g. Swiss Roll.
    Gas Oven: Regulo 8 or H. Electric Oven: 400°F.

Mixtures using melted treacle and syrup (e.g. Gingerbread).
    Gas Oven: Regulo 7 or G. Electric Oven: 350°F.

TIMES FOR COOKING

1. Beef (rib, round or sirloin), 15 to 20 minutes to pound and 20 minutes over.
2. Mutton and Lamb (gigot, shoulder, loin and saddle) 20 minutes to pound and 20 minutes over.
3. Pork (loin, leg or breast), 25 minutes to pound and 25 minutes over.
4. Veal and Lamb, 20 minutes to the pound and 20 minutes over.
5. Chicken, 1 hour to 1½ hours, according to age.

   Joints under 3 lbs. require longer time in proportion.

Mutton, Veal and Pork must be served thoroughly cooked. Beef can be served underdone.

BAKING

Baking is cooking in hot air in the same way as roasting. Suitable for fish, pies, puddings, fruit, scones, etc

INSTRUCTIONS

1. Arrange position of shelves in oven. Heat oven.
   If heated by coal, allow 1 hour.
   If heated by oil, allow 1 hour.
   If heated by gas, allow 20 to 25 minutes.
   If heated by electricity, 30 to 40 minutes.
2. Do not open oven door more than necessary.

To test oven heat.   Moderate oven. White paper should brown in 2 minutes.
Hot oven. White paper should brown in 1½ minutes.

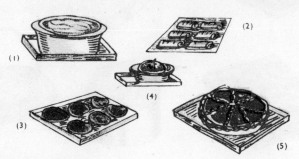

1. Baked Bread-and-butter Pudding.
2. Sausage Rolls.   3. Baked Potatoes.
4. Baked Apple.   5. Baked Jam Tart.

BAKING FOR TEA

Aim. To serve light, well-cooked, appetizing dishes.
1. Loaf tin.   2. Flat baking-sheet.   3. Fluted baking-cases.   4. Baking-tin.   5. Sheet of patty tins.   6. Sandwich tin.   7. Girdle.   8. Palette knife.   9. Wooden Spoon.   10. Whisk 11. Flour dredger.

(a) Loaf.   (c) Queen cakes.   (e) Sponge sandwich.   (g) Cake.
(b) Oven scones.   (d) London buns.   (f) Jam tartlets.   (h) Potato scones.

SOUP-MAKING

1. Choose a deep pan with a tight-fitting lid.
2. Prepare stock carefully.
3. Allow half-pint per person, and always make enough for two days.
4. Use equal quantities of vegetables so that no special flavour predominates except that which gives the soup its name.
5. Season carefully.
6. Remove scum from vegetable soups.
7. Cook gently for a long period.

FOR PREPARATION OF
VEGETABLES (SEE PAGE 35)

BONE STOCK

Stock is the liquid in which bones, meat, fish and vegetables have been boiled.
Aim. To draw out as much flavour as possible.

Recipe.

2 lbs bones.	1 carrot
2 qts. water	$\frac{1}{2}$ turnip
1 dessertspoon salt	1 onion

WASH BONES AND
REMOVE FAT

PLACE BONES IN PAN
WITH ENOUGH WATER TO COVER
ADD SALT.   BRING SLOWLY TO
THE BOIL AND SIMMER GENTLY
FOR SEVERAL HOURS.   ADD
VEGETABLES, CUT UP
ROUGHLY TWO
HOURS BEFORE
STOCK IS DUE
TO FINISH COOKING.

STRAIN INTO A BOWL
AND USE AS
A FOUNDATION FOR
SOUPS, GRAVY, ETC.

POTATO SOUP

Recipe.
4 or 5 large potatoes
2 pints stock
I onion
I grated carrot

Place stock in
pan and allow
to simmer.

Add potatoes
sliced thinly, carrot
grated, and onion
chopped finely.
Add salt and pepper, put on lid and
simmer gently for 1½ to 2 hours.
Prepare parsley (see page 36).
Pour soup into hot tureen, stir
in parsley and serve hot.

SCOTCH BROTH

Recipe. I tablespoonful peas   I carrot
I tablespoonful barley   I small turnip
I dessertspoonful salt   I onion
I quart water   ¼ cabbage
I lb. boiling beef   I leek
or mutton   Parsley, pepper

Wash and
steep peas
overnight.
Wash and scald barley.
Put peas, barley, salt and
cold water in pan.
Bring to the boil.

Wipe meat and add to boiling water.
Prepare vegetables (page 35) and
add to broth. Dice root vegetables
and shred green vegetables.
Put on lid and simmer soup steadily for
2 hours, add pepper. Chop parsley
(page 36). Pour soup into hot tureen,
stir in parsley and serve hot.

20

LENTIL SOUP.

Recipe.

6 ozs. lentils	½ oz. dripping,
I qt. water.	margarine, etc.
I potato	Salt
I carrot	Shake pepper
½ small turnip	Parsley (chopped)
I onion.	

Wash and steep lentils overnight. Measure fat into pan and bring to smoking-hot temperature. Fry lentils in fat. Place lid on and stir frequently. Add water and prepared vegetables.. Simmer for 2 to 3 hours. Add salt and pepper. Prepare parsley (**see** page 36). Pour soup into hot tureen. Stir parsley and serve hot.

KIDNEY SOUP.

Recipe.

½ ox kidney.	I oz. dripping.
Piece turnip.	I quart stock.
Piece carrot.	Seasoning.
I small onion.	½ oz. cornflour.
I stick celery.	

Method. Wash skin and remove fat from kidney. Cut in dice. Dip in flour. Prepare vegetables. Cut in fairly large pieces. Chop onion. Measure fat into pan. Fry kidney till brown. Fry vegetables. Add stock or water. Add seasoning. Cook gently for 2 to 3 hours. Heat the tureen. Strain soup into a bowl. Return liquid to pan with the kidney. Blend cornflour with enough water to make a smooth, creamy consistency, using a wooden spoon. Pour into soup, stirring all the time with wooden spoon till soup boils. Simmer for 5 to 10 minutes. Pour into tureen. Serve hot.

MUTTON BROTH.

For Invalids.

Method. Wipe meat, cut in small pieces and remove fat. Place in pan with cold water and salt. Leave for a short time then bring slowly to boil. Simmer slowly. Heat small serving bowl or soup cup. Prepare vegetables and cut up roughly. Add to soup and leave to simmer for 3 hours. Pour soup through sieve and return to pan. Wash sago and sprinkle in, stirring with a wooden spoon. Cook 20 to 30 minutes. Serve daintily.

Recipe.

I lb. lean mutton.
2 pints water.
Salt.
I small onion.
I small carrot.
Piece turnip.
1½ ozs. sago, or I tablespoon cornflour.

NOTE. Chicken Broth is made in the same way.

TOMATO SOUP.

Recipe.   I lb. tomatoes.   2 ozs. bacon rind.   Seasoning.
                    Piece carrot. $\frac{1}{2}$ teaspoon sugar.   I quart stock.
                    Piece onion. $\frac{1}{2}$ oz. margarine. $\frac{1}{2}$ oz. cornflour.

Method. Slice tomatoes and vegetables. Place in soup pan with margarine, sugar, bacon rind and seasoning. Stir together in pan with wooden spoon for 5 to 10 minutes. Add stock, cover with lid and simmer gently for $\frac{3}{4}$ hour. Heat soup tureen. Rub soup through sieve into a bowl and measure the amount of liquid strained. Return soup to pan. Thicken with cornflour, allowing $\frac{1}{4}$ oz. cornflour to I pint liquid. Place cornflour in bowl and blend with water till smooth and creamy. Pour into pan and stir with wooden spoon till boiling. Simmer 10 minutes. Pour into tureen and serve hot.

FISH DISHES.
Choosing Fish.

1. Fresh fish should have a pleasant smell, plenty of scales, red gills and bright eyes.
2. Choose them firm and thick with plenty of flesh.
3. There are three classes of fish:—
    1. White Fish, e.g., haddock, sole, cod, halibut, etc.
    2. Oily Fish, e.g., herring, salmon, mackerel.
    3. Shell Fish, e.g., oysters, crabs, lobsters.

White Fish is light and digestible. The oil is contained in the liver which is removed during cleaning. They are best cooked with fat to make up for this lack of fat.

Oily Fish. The oil is present throughout the body, therefore it is more indigestible. It is usually served with lemon or vinegar as an accompaniment. This helps to counteract the richness. Grilling is a suitable method for cooking oily fish. The internal organs of the fish generally used are herring and cod's roe.

Shell Fish are very indigestible and should only be eaten very fresh.

Tests for Readiness.
1. The flesh should leave the bone.
2. A white curd oozes from flesh when fish is cooked.
3. The skin should come away easily.

METHOD OF PREPARING A COATING BATTER.

For frying Filletted Haddock, etc.,
and Fish Cakes and Meat Cakes.

       Recipe.   I tablespoon flour.
                   $\frac{1}{2}$ teaspoon salt.
                   Shake pepper.
                   A little milk.
                      breadcrumbs.

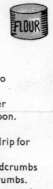

Method. Measure flour into bowl. Add salt and pepper. Mix to a smooth creamy batter with milk, using a wooden spoon. Have fish washed and dried. Dip fish into batter. Allow to drip for a second.

Lay on paper with white breadcrumbs or bread raspings. Toss in crumbs. Shake fish gently. Lay on plate ready for frying.

NOTE. Crumbs are not necessary.

TO PREPARE FISH CAKES OR MEAT CAKES

Method. Make panada in same way as a white sauce (page 42). The result should be a very thick sauce, which should leave the sides of the pan.
Flake fish and remove bones.
Mash potato and prepare bread-crumbs. Add all to panada, with seasoning and beat well. Lay aside to cool and stiffen round edge of plate.
Flour board and shape mixture into rounds ½-inch thick. Beat egg and pour on to plate. Lay white paper on board and spread with breadcrumbs or bread raspings. Dip fish cakes in egg and brush with pastry brush. Turn with knife and brush other side and also edges. Toss in breadcrumbs then shake off loose crumbs gently. Lay on plate ready for frying.
NOTE. For salmon croquettes use a small tin salmon.

Recipe. Panada (very thick white sauce).
1½ ozs. flour.
1 oz. margarine.
1 gill milk.
Seasoning.
½ lb. cooked fish or meat.
1 tablespoon bread-crumbs.
2 tablesp. cooked potato.

BOILED COD.

Recipe.
1 or 2 lbs cod.
1 tablespoon salt to 1 qt. water.
1 tablespoon vinegar.
Parsley.
Pieces of lemon.

Method. Heat ashet. Heat water in fish kettle. Scale, wash and dry fish. Put on in boiling water. Add salt and vinegar. Keep under boiling point and allow 6 minutes to each pound and 6 minutes over. Remove fish and drain. Serve on a hot ashet with slices of lemon and parsley. Serve with a white sauce.
NOTE. **Salmon** may be boiled in this way. Add ½ lemon in place of vinegar. Boil gently (2 lbs. will take about ½ hour). Serve cold with parsley, slices of cucumber and cut lemon.

POTTED OR SOUSED HERRING.

Recipe. 1 herring.
Salt and pepper.
½ gill water.
½ gill vinegar.
A few bay leaves.
3 or 4 peppercorns.

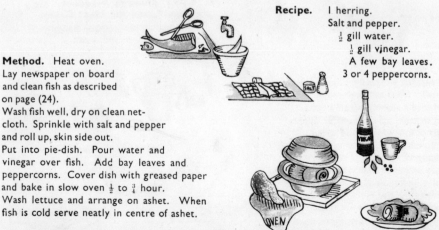

Method. Heat oven. Lay newspaper on board and clean fish as described on page (24).
Wash fish well, dry on clean net-cloth. Sprinkle with salt and pepper and roll up, skin side out.
Put into pie-dish. Pour water and vinegar over fish. Add bay leaves and peppercorns. Cover dish with greased paper and bake in slow oven ½ to ¾ hour.
Wash lettuce and arrange on ashet. When fish is cold serve neatly in centre of ashet.

FRIED FILLETTED HADDOCK.

½ lb. filletted haddock.
breadcrumbs.
batter (page 92).
1½ to 2 lbs. fat.
lemon.
parsley.

Method. Heat ashet.
Have dish-paper ready,
also tray with draining
paper.
Place basket in unlined pan,
add fat and heat slowly.
Have a lid handy in case of fire. (page 15)
Prepare fish and coat with batter,
add breadcrumbs (page 22). Shake
off loose crumbs and lay fish on plate.
When fat is faintly smoking, lift basket and
place fish in it. Lower basket slowly into
fat. Fry till **golden-brown,** raise basket for
a second and allow to drip, turn fish on to
draining paper then serve on hot ashet with
dish-paper.
Decorate with cut lemon and parsley.

FRIED HERRING.

2 herrings.
1 tablespoon oatmeal.
¼ teaspoon salt.
Shake pepper.
Fat to fry.
parsley.

Method.
Heat ashet.
Prepare seasoned
oatmeal. Lay news-
paper on board. Trim
tail, fins, gills, etc.
Remove head, clean out
internal organs, keeping roe
if any, for frying. Slit fish down
front with scissors. Lay flat out and run the
thumb under back-bone on both sides and
bone away. Clean herring on both sides
with salt to remove black inside skin and
also scales. Wash fish and dry on clean
netcloth. Dip in seasoned oatmeal. Shake
and fry in smoking hot fat on both sides
frying skin side first. Cook thoroughly
and serve hot.

GRILLED KIPPER.

Lay kipper on news-
paper. Remove head and
tail. Wipe. Heat grill, lay kipper
on trivet, place under grill and
cook for 10 minutes on both sides till
flesh begins to come away from bone.
Serve quickly on hot ashet.

FRIED COD STEAK.

Heat ashet.
Collect dish-paper
Scrape off scales.
Wash fish and dry on
netcloth. Prepare batter and
crumbs and coat fish (page 22).
Shake off loose crumbs. Heat fat
till faintly smoking. Fry fish on both sides
till well-cooked and golden-brown. Lift on to
draining-paper then serve on hot ashet with dish-paper. Decorate
with cut lemon and parsley.

BAKED FILLETTED HADDOCK.

Recipe. 2 filletted haddocks.
Salt and pepper.
butter.
Milk.
parsley.

Method.
Heat oven.
Heat ashet and
prepare parsley.
Grease paper for top
of tin.
Wash fish well in cold
water. Dry. Place on net-
cloth and sprinkle with seasoning. Roll up tail to head,
skin side inside.
Butter the bottom of a dripping-
tin. Lay fillets on end as shown.
Put a pat of butter on each one.
Add a little milk to cover bottom
of tin. Cover with greased paper
and bake in a slow oven 20 mins.
till flakes begin to separate.
Lift on to hot ashet with fish
slice. Decorate tops with
parsley. Serve hot with white
sauce (page 42).
NOTE. Use milk from baked fish as
   part of liquid in making the white sauce.

BAKED FISH CUSTARD.

Recipe.   1 filletted whiting.   Salt and pepper.
                   $\frac{1}{2}$ egg.   Parsley.
                   1 gill milk.

Method. Heat oven. Grease pie-dish. Wash fish in cold water. Dry and lay on netcloth. Sprinkle skin side with salt and pepper. Roll up, tail to head. Lay in pie-dish on end. Beat egg slightly with a fork. Add milk and seasoning. Pour round fish and bake in a moderate oven for 30 minutes or until fish is cooked and custard sets. Decorate with parsley. Serve hot.

STEAMED FILLETTED WHITING.
(Invalid Dish).

Recipe. 1 filletted whiting.
            $\frac{1}{2}$ oz. butter.
            Salt and pepper.
            Parsley.

Method.
Heat water in pan. Butter the plate. Wash fish well. Lay on clean net-cloth and dry. Sprinkle skin side with salt and very little pepper. Roll up, tail to head. Lay whiting on plate. Place a pat of butter on top of fish. Place plate on pan and cover with a bowl. Steam 20 to 25 minutes till fish flakes begin to separate. Remove from pan and wipe bottom of plate. Decorate with parsley. Serve neatly.

SALMON MOULD.

Recipe.   1 teacup breadcrumbs.   Seasoning.
                   1 teacup milk. $\frac{1}{2}$ lb. tin salmon.
                   $\frac{1}{2}$ oz. butter.   1 egg.

Method. Heat ashet. Grease bowl and paper. Boil water in pan. (See steaming page 12). Grate bread into bowl. Warm milk and butter in pan. Pour over breadcrumbs in bowl. Add tinned salmon, salt and pepper. Beat egg, add to mixture, pour into prepared bowl and steam for $\frac{1}{2}$ an hour. Turn on to ashet and serve hot.

NOTE. Any cooked fish may be flaked, bones removed and added in place of salmon.

KEDGEREE.

Recipe.   ¼ lb. boiled rice.   Lemon.
                  ½ lb. cooked fish.   Parsley.
                  ½ oz. margarine.   Salt and pepper.
                  1 egg.

Method. Heat ashet. Hard-boil 1 egg. (Put on in a pan of cold water, bring to boil and boil 10 minutes. Plunge in cold water). Shell and chop. Flake fish and remove bones and skin. Put fish on plate. Chop parsley. Prepare lemon butterflies (see page 50). Melt margarine in pan. Add fish, cooked rice, chopped egg, salt and pepper. Heat thoroughly in pan, stirring well with wooden spoon. Turn on to hot ashet. Pile up neatly and sprinkle with parsley. Decorate with lemon butterflies. Serve very hot.

MEAT.
How to Choose Meat.

Meat should smell fresh and be firm to the touch and not too moist.

Flesh should be bright red and of a close texture in beef, dark red in mutton and pink in lamb, veal and pork.

The fat should be white in mutton, lamb and pork and a deep cream in beef.

Imported frozen meat should be thawed slowly before cooking.

Chicken. Breast bone should bend slightly and a chicken should have smooth legs and feet.

Rabbit. Should be plump—flesh, clear and pale. Choose a young rabbit for roasting and an older one for boiling, steaming and stewing.

Choose suitable cuts of meat for method of cooking to be used.

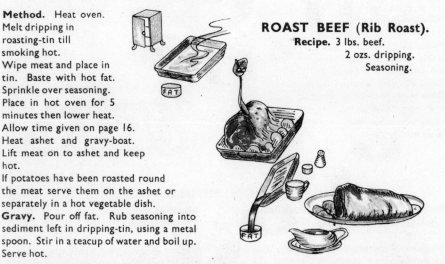

Method. Heat oven. Melt dripping in roasting-tin till smoking hot. Wipe meat and place in tin. Baste with hot fat. Sprinkle over seasoning. Place in hot oven for 5 minutes then lower heat. Allow time given on page 16. Heat ashet and gravy-boat. Lift meat on to ashet and keep hot.

If potatoes have been roasted round the meat serve them on the ashet or separately in a hot vegetable dish.

Gravy. Pour off fat. Rub seasoning into sediment left in dripping-tin, using a metal spoon. Stir in a teacup of water and boil up. Serve hot.

ROAST BEEF (Rib Roast).
Recipe. 3 lbs. beef.
            2 ozs. dripping.
            Seasoning.

ROAST MUTTON. This is cooked in the same way as beef, allowing time given on page 17. Gravy for mutton is thickened, using 1 dessertspoon flour. Pour off fat and rub flour into sediment in dripping-tin. Add seasoning. Pour in a teacup of water and boil up. Serve hot.

BOILED SALT MEAT.

Soak meat
in cold water
for a few hours.
Heat ashet.
Put meat into pan
with water and cover
with lid and bring to
the boil. Pour off water.
Put meat into pan again
and cover with boiling water
put on lid and simmer gently,
allowing 30 minutes to the pound
and 30 minutes over. Prepare
carrots and cut into neat pieces.
Add to pan ½ to ¾ hour before meat
is due to finish cooking. Prepare
savoury dumplings (page 93) and add
to pan. Serve on hot ashet, meat in
centre, carrots and dumplings round.
NOTE. All salt meats are boiled
similarly. For pickled pork and ham,
remove skin and sprinkle with raspings.

Recipe.   3 lbs. salt beef.
            1 lb. carrots.
            Savoury dumplings.
             (page 93).

TO BOIL TRIPE.

Wash tripe well in warm water. Place in pan, cover
with water and heat till almost boiling. Drain and
scrape tripe on board with a knife. Put on with fresh
cold water and simmer 6 to 9 hours. When tender,
strain liquid (keep liquid for
stock) and cut tripe
in neat pieces.

STEWED TRIPE AND ONIONS.

Boil tripe as above and cut up. Place in pan, and
cover with milk. Season and add sliced onions.
Simmer for 1 hour. Blend flour with a
little cold milk and add to hot liquid
in pan, stirring till it boils. Heat
ashet. Make toast and
cut in pieces. Serve
hot on toast.

Recipe.
2 lbs. tripe.
Salt and pepper.
4 onions.
1 pint milk.
1 tablespoon flour.
1 slice toast.

28

STEWED MINCE.

Method.
Heat ashet.
Cut onion in
thin slices.
Melt dripping in
pan, add mince and
onion and stir well
with a fork till mince is
brown. Add water, place
lid on pan and simmer for
20 to 30 minutes. Blend seasoned
flour with water till creamy and
pour into mince. Stir till boiling
and sprinkle in oatmeal.
Make toast and cut in pieces.
Serve mince on hot ashet with toast
around.

Recipe.
½ lb. mince.
1 small onion.
½ gill water.
¼ oz. dripping.
1 dessertspoon flour.
Seasoning.
1 slice toast.

STEWED RABBIT.

Recipe.
1 rabbit.
1 oz. dripping.
1 onion.
1 tablespoon seasoned
    flour.
Salt and pepper.
1 pint water.
1 carrot.

Method.
Skin rabbit and
wash. Remove heart,
lungs, kidney and liver.
Soak rabbit in warm
salted water for ½ hour.
Dry and cut into neat joints.
Dip in seasoned flour. Have
dripping smoking hot, fry onion
rings till golden brown then fry
rabbit. Add water or stock and stir
till boiling. Simmer for 1½ to 2 hours,
adding rings of carrot. Cook till tender.
Heat ashet. Serve hot.

IRISH STEW.

Recipe.   ½ lb. shoulder mutton.
4 or 5 large potatoes.
2 onions.
I gill boiling water.
Seasoning.

Method.
Wipe meat and
cut in suitable
sizes and place in
pan.
Chop onion in rings.
Slice one potato finely.
Place onion and potato
over meat.
Measure boiling water and
pour over meat and vegetables.
Add seasoning. Simmer for I
hour, stirring occasionally.
Slice remaining potatoes in ½ in.
slices. Add to top of stew and
simmer ½ hour longer.
After adding the thick slices of
potato avoid stirring the stew as this
breaks up the potato. Shake pan
instead.
Serve on hot ashet, meat in centre, vegetables round.

STEWED STEAK AND VEGETABLES.

Recipe.   I onion.
½ lb. stewing steak.
I dessertspoon flour.
½ teaspoon salt.
Shake pepper.
I gill water.
I carrot.
Piece turnip.

Method.
Heat ashet.
Prepare onion
and cut in rings.
Wipe meat and cut
in 2 inch strips.
Measure flour, salt
and pepper on to
plate, and dip meat
into this seasoned flour.
Have water measured ready.
Fry onion for 2 minutes, add
meat and any seasoned flour left on plate.
Fry till brown (2 or 3 minutes on each side).
Add water, bring to the boil, lower heat and allow
stew to simmer gently 1½ to 2 hours. Add prepared
vegetables cut neatly, about ½ hour before stew is due to
finish cooking.
Serve hot on ashet with vegetables round.

STEAMED MEAT ROLL.

Recipe. ½ lb. mince.
2 ozs. chopped bacon.
I teacup breadcrumbs.
I dessertspoon milk.
Chopped parsley.
¼ teaspoon salt.
Shake pepper.
½ egg.
Bread raspings.

Method.
Grease a
straight-sided
jelly jar, also paper
to cover. Heat water
in pan as on page 12.
Heat ashet. Grate bread,
chop parsley and add to mince
in bowl. Beat egg thoroughly
and add milk. Add to ingredients
in bowl and mix well. Season and
arrange mixture in jelly-jar.
Cover and steam 1½ hours.
Spread some bread raspings on a
sheet of white paper. Turn out
meat roll and coat with raspings.
Serve on hot ashet or cold, on a
bed of crisp lettuce.

STEAMED MEAT PUDDING.

(Steaming page 12).
Recipe. Few cooked vegetables.
¼ lb. steak.
½ sheeps kidney.
Seasoned—I teaspoon flour.
flour.   —¼ teaspoon salt.
—Shake pepper.
I tablespoon water.
3 ozs. suet crust pastry.

Grease
bowl and
paper. Heat
water in pan.
Dice vegetables.
Wash kidney, skin
and remove core and
fat and chop in small pieces.
Wipe meat and cut in ½-in. strips.
Dip kidney and meat in seasoned
flour. Roll up meat. Put kidney
and meat on a plate. Prepare suet
pastry (page 45). Flour board. Turn pastry
cn to board. Cut off a small piece to cover
pudding. Roll large piece into round ¼-in. thick.
Line bowl with this pastry. Fill with meat and diced vegetables.
Add water. Damp top edges and lay on round of pastry for the top.
Seal edges. Cover with greased paper and steam 2 to 3 hours.
Turn on to hot ashet, make a hole in top and pour in a little boiling water.

STEAMED CHOP.
(Invalid Dish.)
Recipe.   1 chop.
          Salt.

Method.
Half fill pan with
water for steaming.
Wipe chop and remove
outer layer of fat with a
knife.
Place chop on a plate to
fit top of pan and sprinkle
lightly with salt. Lay
another plate on top to
cover, place over boiling
water in pan and steam
till tender, turning occasionally,
about 1-1½ hours. Remove plate, wipe
underneath and serve neatly.

SAUSAGE ROLLS.
Recipe.   2 sausages.
          3 ozs. rough puff pastry.
          egg to brush.
          parsley.

Method.
Heat oven.
Wipe sausages,
skin and cut in halves.
Prepare pastry as on
page 46. Roll out to ¼-inch
thickness. Divide pastry into
4 pieces. Lay sausage on each
piece. Damp half way round edge
of pastry. Fold pastry over and press
edges lightly together. Flake edges
horizontally with knife. Make two slits
in each sausage roll. Lay on baking tin and
brush top with egg.
Bake in a hot oven about ½ hour till well risen,
crisp and golden-brown.
Serve on a hot ashet and decorate with parsley.

CORNISH PASTY.

Recipe.   3 ozs. short crust pastry.
2 ozs. cooked meat.
I small potato.
I small onion.
Salt and pepper.
egg to brush.
parsley.

Method.
Heat oven.
Have potato cooked,
also onion. Chop in
rough pieces on plate.
Remove fat and skin from
the meat. Chop meat and
season. Prepare pastry as on
page 46. Roll into a round $\frac{1}{4}$-inch
thick. Lay pastry half over rolling-
pin and arrange meat and vegetables
in centre Damp half-way round edge of
pastry and press edges together.
Decorate edge in rope design with the fingers.
Make two slits with the knife. Place on a
baking-tin and brush with egg or milk.
Bake in a fairly hot oven about $\frac{1}{2}$ hour till crisp, golden-
brown and well-cooked. Serve either hot or cold.
Decorate with parsley.

STEAK AND KIDNEY PIE.

Recipe.
$\frac{1}{4}$ lb. stewing steak.
I sheep's kidney.
$\frac{1}{4}$ oz. flour.
Salt and pepper.
4 ozs. rough puff
pastry.
egg to brush.
parsley.

Method.
Heat oven.
Wipe meat and
cut in thin slices,
dip in seasoned flour
and roll up. Place on
end in pie-dish. Wash
kidney, skin, remove core and
cut in pieces. Place a piece of
kidney on top of each roll of steak.
Prepare pastry (page 46) and roll out
to $\frac{1}{4}$-inch thickness. Have pastry a size
larger than pie-dish. Cut off a strip all round,
the width of the rim of the pie-dish. Damp rim of pie-
dish and lay on the strip, joining the edges by damping
one edge. Damp strip. Lay remaining pastry on top to cover pie.
Press edges lightly together. Trim edges all round with knife. Flake edges of pastry by holding
knife horizontally. Use scraps of pastry to make leaves by cutting diamond shapes and flaking
edges with knife. Make a hole in the centre of pie and damp round about. Lay leaves neatly
round the hole. Brush top of pie with egg, place pie on tray and bake in a hot oven 10 to 15
minutes to set pastry then lower heat and bake slowly about 2 hours till meat is tender.
Decorate with parsley.

VEGETABLE PIE.

Filling.

2 tomatoes.	I small cooked potato.
2 tablespoons cooked beans.	I tablespoon chopped parsley.
Pieces of cooked carrot.	Salt and pepper.
Pieces of cooked turnip.	2 tablespoons stock or water.
I small cooked onion.	

Method. Slice tomatoes and potatoes. Dice carrot and turnip. Chop onion. Place in layers
with salt and pepper and parsley, add stock. Cover as shown.

C

SHEPHERD'S PIE.

¼ lb. cooked meat or cooked mince.
¼ oz. dripping.
¼ oz. flour.
I small onion.
I gill water.
pepper and salt.
2 potatoes.
I tablespoon milk.

Method.
Put potatoes
on to cook. Prepare
gravy as follows:—
Heat dripping till smoking hot.
Fry onion till brown; then fry
flour. Add water gradually and
stir till boiling. Season, add meat
(chopped and free from gristle) and stir.
Place meat and gravy in pie-dish. Beat
potatoes with milk and seasoning. Place
neatly over meat in pie-dish and decorate
with a fork. Place pie-dish on baking-tin
and re-heat in a moderately hot oven till
brown on top. Place pie-dish on an ashet.
Serve hot.

CURRY OF COLD MEAT.

Recipe.

½ lb. cooked meat.   ½ oz. flour.
I oz. butter.   Few drips of lemon juice.
I apple.   Salt and pepper.
I small onion.   ½ pint stock or water.
I teaspoon curry powder.

Method. Heat ashet. Chop apple and onion. Melt butter in pan. Fry onion, apple, curry powder and flour together; stirring with a wooden spoon. Cook for about 10 minutes. Add stock slowly, stirring well. Add salt, pepper and lemon juice and continue stirring till stock boils. Simmer for 20 minutes. Cut meat into neat pieces, add to sauce and reheat. Serve on hot ashet with boiled rice (page 92) round.

TOAD IN A HOLE.

Method. Heat oven. Prepare batter as on page 92 and leave aside to cool. Grease pie-dish. Wipe 2 sausages and skin. Cut in halves and place in pie-dish. Pour over enough batter to half-fill pie-dish. Place pie-dish on a baking tray and bake in a moderately hot oven ½ hour till well risen and cooked. Place pie-dish on an ashet and serve hot.

YORKSHIRE PUDDING.

Heat oven. Prepare batter as on page 92. Melt ½ oz. dripping in dripping tin. Pour in batter. Bake in a moderate hot oven ½ hour till well risen and cooked. Divide in 6 or **8** pieces and serve on a hot ashet.

VEGETABLES.

1. **Root,** e.g., potatoes, turnip, parsnip, beetroot, etc., contain starch.
2. **Green,** e.g., cabbage, lettuce, onions, parsley, contain mineral salts and vitamins.
3. **Pulses,** e.g., lentils, peas, beans, contain protein and starch.

CHOICE OF VEGETABLES.

Vegetable should feel firm and be fresh. Green vegetables should be crisp and a good colour. Pulse vegetables should be fresh with a clean smell.

Vegetables are best cooked by methods using fat as they lack fat. Boiling is a watery method and very tasteless. Valuable salts are drained away.

THE CONSERVATIVE METHOD (PAGE 37) IS THE BEST METHOD OF COOKING ROOT AND GREEN VEGETABLES.

PREPARATION OF VEGETABLES.

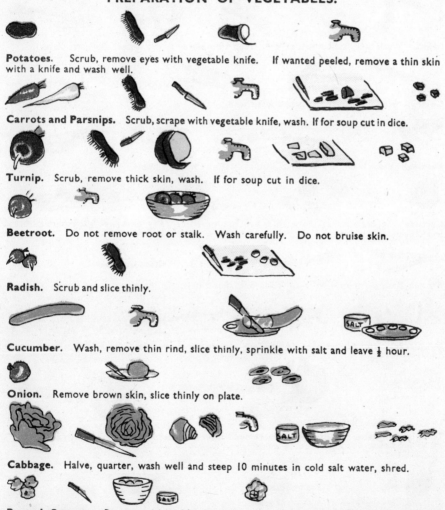

Potatoes. Scrub, remove eyes with vegetable knife. If wanted peeled, remove a thin skin with a knife and wash well.

Carrots and Parsnips. Scrub, scrape with vegetable knife, wash. If for soup cut in dice.

Turnip. Scrub, remove thick skin, wash. If for soup cut in dice.

Beetroot. Do not remove root or stalk. Wash carefully. Do not bruise skin.

Radish. Scrub and slice thinly.

Cucumber. Wash, remove thin rind, slice thinly, sprinkle with salt and leave ½ hour.

Onion. Remove brown skin, slice thinly on plate.

Cabbage. Halve, quarter, wash well and steep 10 minutes in cold salt water, shred.

Brussels Sprouts. Remove withered leaves, wash, steep 10 minutes in cold salt water. Cut a cross on end of stack.

Cauliflower. Trim off leaves, wash well and steep 10 minutes in cold salt water.

Peas and Beans. Shell.

Leeks. Wash well, split down centre, steep 10 minutes in salt water. Slice on plate.

Celery. Scrub, separate stalks and wash well.

Parsley. Wash well, dry in towel, remove staiks and chop heads.

Lettuce. Separate leaves and wash under running water. Lay on towel, gather up corners and shake well.

French Beans. Remove thread, wash and slice thinly, slantwise.

Watercress and Fine Cress. Wash and place on towel to dry.

To Skin Tomatoes. Pour boiling water over, leave for a second and plunge into cold water.

Lentils, Peas and Beans. Wash in several cold waters. Steep overnight in cold water.

CONSERVATIVE METHOD OF COOKING VEGETABLES

Suitable for Root and Green Vegetables.

The Aim, is to " conserve " or keep in the goodness.

Instructions.

Use a vessel with a tight fitting lid, e.g., stewpan, casserole or pyrex dish. Prepare vegetables (pages 35 & 36). Put fat and water in pan and heat, add vegetables. Sprinkle with salt and a shake of pepper. Place lid on and cook very slowly till tender. Careful attention is necessary to prevent contents of pan from burning. Shake pan frequently and serve with liquid.

Proportions.

2 lbs. vegetables. $\frac{1}{2}$ oz. fat.
1 teaspoon salt. $\frac{1}{2}$ gill water.

WAYS OF COOKING POTATOES.

Aim. To have well-cooked and floury.

Choose potatoes of an even size. Scrub, remove thin skin and any eyes and wash. Potatoes retain more nourishment if cooked in their skins.

1. **Steamed** (See page 12). Sprinkle with salt and cook 30 to 40 minutes till soft. Test with a fork. Serve in hot vegetable dish with chopped parsley sprinkled over.

2. **Baked.** Scrub well, prick with a fork and bake in a moderate oven about 45 minutes or till tender.

3. **Roasted.** Melt $\frac{1}{2}$ oz. dripping in a roasting tin till smoking hot. Place potatoes in fat and roast in a hot oven till soft, turning occasionally till golden-brown.
   Drain and serve in a hot vegetable dish. The potatoes may be roasted with the joint.

4. **Boiled.** Scrub well and put on in boiling water, using 1 dessertspoon salt to 1 quart water. Boil 25 minutes till tender. Test with fork. Drain and serve hot in vegetable dish.

FRIED POTATO CHIPS.

Recipe:

2 or 3 potatoes (large).

2 lbs. fat (dripping or lard).

salt and pepper.

Method.

Prepare potatoes, peel, slice thickly then cut in lengths. Steep in cold water 20 to 30 minutes. Heat fat over a low flame with a basket in pan. Have a lid ready in case of emergency. Dry potatoes on towel and lay on plate. Heat vegetable dish. When fat is smoking hot, lift basket and place a few chips in carefully. Lower basket and fry till golden brown. Drain on paper, sprinkle with salt and pepper and keep hot while frying remaining chips. Serve in hot vegetable dish.

BOILED HARICOT BEANS OR PEAS.

Recipe. ½ lb. haricot beans.

1 oz. butter.

salt and pepper.

parsley (chopped).

Method.

Wash beans and steep overnight in cold water. Place in pan of boiling water Boil for 2 hours or until soft. Drain and return to pan. Add salt, add 1 oz. butter and more seasoning if necessary. Shake pan. Add chopped parsley and shake again. Serve hot in vegetable dish.

BOILED BEETROOT.
Recipe.

1 lb. beetroot.   salt.
Boiling water to cover.

Method.
Wash beet-
root well. Be
careful not to
break the skin.
Put into a pan of
boiling water and
boil till tender.
Do not prick, test
by pressing with the
fingers.   Plunge beet-
roots in cold water.
Skin and slice. Serve in
hot vegetable dish with
white sauce (page 42)
poured over or cold with
vinegar in a glass dish.
NOTE.   Beetroot may be pickled.   Boil 1 gill vinegar
and 1 gill water with a few peppercorns. Cool and
pour over beetroot in jar.

MASHED TURNIP.
Recipe.

1 turnip.
water to cover.
salt.
$\frac{1}{2}$ oz. butter.
seasoning.
parsley.

Method.
Prepare turnip
(page 35) and cut in
pieces. Put on to boil
with enough boiling
water to cover, add salt
boil till tender ($\frac{1}{2}$ to $\frac{3}{4}$
hour).   Turnip may be
steamed instead, in which
case allow an hour for cooking.
Heat vegetable dish.   Chop
parsley. Drain turnip and mash
till creamy with butter and seasoning.   Arrange neatly in vegetable dish and sprinkle parsley over.

GARDEN PEAS.

I lb. peas.
I oz. butter.
I level teaspoon sugar.
Sprig of mint.
½ teaspoon salt.
Shake of pepper.
½ gill boiling water.

Method.
Shell peas.
Heat oven.
Put peas in cas-
serole with mint
(well washed) sugar,
salt and pepper.
Pour boiling water
over and cover with
lid. Cook gently till
peas are tender
(about 20 minutes).
Remove mint. Serve
hot in casserole.

ROASTED ONIONS.

Recipe—3 or 4 Spanish onions.
½ oz. dripping or margarine.
salt.

Method.
Prepare onions. Put in boiling salted water and boil till tender, about 2 hours. Heat fat in roasting tin. Drain onions and place in hot fat. Roast in oven till brown. Serve in hot vegetable dish with melted butter.

BOILED ONIONS IN WHITE SAUCE.

Recipe.
3 or 4 spanish onions.
½ pint white sauce.
salt.

Method.
Boil onions as above. Heat vegetable dish.
Make white sauce (page 42). Drain onions
and place in vegetable dish. Pour sauce over
and serve hot.
NOTE. Celery can be cooked and served in
the same way.

CAULIFLOWER WITH CHEESE SAUCE.

Recipe.
1 Cauliflower.
salt.
½ pint white sauce.
2-3 ozs. cheese.
parsley.

Method.
Prepare vegetable steamer over pan of soup or boiling water
Prepare cauliflower (page 36). Place in steamer, flower up, sprinkle with salt and steam till tender. Heat oven. Grate cheese for sauce. Make sauce (page 42) and season well. Add half the cheese and stir well. Arrange cauliflower in casserole or glass pyrex dish, pour sauce over top and sprinkle with rest of cheese. Place in oven to brown the cheese. Chop parsley and sprinkle over top. Serve in casserole.
NOTE. The cauliflower may be broken into sprigs and steamed.

ENGLISH SALAD.

1 hard-boiled egg.
1 beetroot (cooked).
2 tomatoes.
1 small carrot.
1 lettuce.
watercress.
fine cress.

Method.
Place egg in pan of cold water and bring slowly to boil. Boil for 10 minutes. Leave in bowl of cold water. When cool, break shell and slice egg.
Prepare tomatoes (as on page 36). Cut in slices. Season, slice beetroot, grate carrot. Prepare lettuce (as on page 36) also watercress and fine cress (page 36).
Arrange salad attractively with the heart of the lettuce in the centre. Serve with salad dressing (page 43).

SAUCES
FOUNDATION WHITE SAUCE.

Aim. To make a smooth, creamy sauce of the correct consistency.

RECIPE.
Coating Sauce.
1 oz. butter   1 oz. flour.
$\frac{1}{2}$ pt. milk.   salt and pepper.

Pouring Sauce.
$\frac{1}{2}$ oz. butter. $\frac{1}{2}$ oz. flour.
$\frac{1}{2}$ pt. milk.   salt and pepper.

VARIETIES:—
Onion Sauce. Add 1 onion (cooked and chopped).
Parsley Sauce. Add 1 tablespoon chopped parsley.
Dutch Sauce. Add yolk of egg and juice of $\frac{1}{2}$ lemon. Re-heat sauce but do not boil.

Method.
Heat sauce-boat. Melt butter in medium-sized pan. Work in flour with a wooden spoon. Cook gently for 1 minute. Measure milk and add very slowly to pan, drop by drop, stirring with the back of a wooden spoon till like thin cream. Put pan over heat and stir well till sauce boils. Cook for 5 minutes, add salt and pepper, pour into sauceboat.
NOTE. A coating sauce should coat the back of the wooden spoon and should be thicker than a pouring sauce.

BROWN SAUCE.

Recipe.
$\frac{1}{2}$ oz. dripping.
1 small onion.
$\frac{1}{2}$ oz. flour.
$\frac{1}{2}$ pint stock or water.
seasoning.
Method. Heat sauce-boat. Have fat smoking hot. Fry onion rings till golden brown. Add liquid and stir till boiling. Boil for 10 minutes strain and serve hot.

APPLE SAUCE.
Recipe.
$\frac{1}{2}$ lb. apples   1 tablespoon water.
$\frac{1}{2}$ oz. sugar.   1 oz. butter.
A few drops lemon juice.
Method. Heat the sauceboat. Prepare apples as for stewing (page 50). Place in pan with sugar and water and stew till soft and pulpy. Beat in butter and lemon juice with a wooden spoon till creamy. Serve in a sauce-boat.

42

TOMATO SAUCE.

Recipe.

I small onion.	½ teaspoon sugar.
I oz. butter.	Seasoning.
4 tomatoes or	I gill stock or water.
I teacup tinned tomato.	½ oz. cornflour.

Method. Heat sauceboat. Chop onion finely, and fry in smoking hot fat. Add tomatoes, **sugar,** seasoning and stock. Bring to the boil and simmer for 20 minutes. Strain into a bowl. **Blend** cornflour with a little water in a cup, pour into bowl, stirring well with a wooden spoon. Return to pan and boil up. Serve hot.

BREAD SAUCE.

Recipe. ½ pint milk.
I small onion.
3 cloves.
6 peppercorns.
I teacup. breadcrumbs
½ oz. butter.
Seasoning.

Method.
Heat sauceboat. Simmer milk for ½ hour with chopped onion, cloves and peppercorns.
Strain and return to pan. Add butter and bread-crumbs and simmer for 5 minutes. Add seasoning and serve hot.

MINT SAUCE.

2 tablespoons boiling water.
¼ oz. sugar.
2 tablespoons chopped mint.
I gill vinegar.

Method. Melt sugar in boiling water. Pour over the chopped mint and when cool, add vinegar. Serve in a sauceboat.

COOKED EGG DRESSING FOR SALADS.

Recipe. I egg.   ½ oz. butter.
I tablespoon vinegar.
I tablespoon milk.
½ teaspoon dry mustard.
I teaspoon sugar.
Salt and pepper.

Method. Beat egg, add all ingredients and mix well in bowl. Stand bowl in pan of hot water and whisk till egg begins to thicken. Serve in a sauceboat.

FRENCH DRESSING.

Recipe. I tablespoon salad oil.
I dessertspoon chopped parsley.
I dessertspoon vinegar.
Salt and pepper.

Method. Stir all ingredients together and mix well. Serve in a sauceboat.

43

CUSTARD SAUCE.
(using egg).

I egg.   ½ pint milk.
½ oz. sugar.

Method. Heat sauceboat. Beat **egg**, add milk and strain into pan. Cook slowly, stirring with a wooden spoon until bottom of pan begins to feel slippery. Remove from heat at once. Add sugar, stir and pour into sauceboat.

CUSTARD SAUCE.
(using custard powder).

Recipe. ½ cz. custard powder.
½ pint milk.
I oz. sugar.

Method. Same as on page 48. Heat sauceboat, make sauce, which should be of a pouring consistency, and serve in sauceboat.

JAM OR MARMALADE SAUCE.

Recipe.   I tablespoonful jam or marmalade.   I gill water.
I tablespoonful sugar.
Juice of ½ lemon.
Method. Boil all together, strain and serve in a sauceboat.

SYRUP SAUCE.

Recipe.   3 tablespoonsful syrup.   3 tablespoonsful lemon juice.
2 tablespoonsful water.
Method. Boil syrup and water. Add lemon juice and serve in a sauceboat.

GENERAL INSTRUCTIONS.

1. Collect all ingredients and utensils before beginning.
2. Make pastry in a cool place.
3. Measure accurately.
4. Work with the tips of the fingers for coolness.
5. Use a knife when mixing pastry.
6. Handle quickly, lightly and as little as possible.
7. Leave aside for a short time to cool, unless baking powder is to be used, in which case the pastry must be cooked immediately.

SUET CRUST PASTRY.

Aim. To make light, spongy and well-cooked.

4 ozs. flour.
2 ozs. suet.
$\frac{1}{4}$ teaspoonful baking powder.
$\frac{1}{4}$ teaspoonful salt.
Cold water.

$\frac{1}{4}$ teaspoon.
B. Powder.

Method.

If pastry is to be steamed prepare pan, bowl and paper (page 12) or heat oven for baking.

Measure flour into bowl prepare the suet (skin, shred and chop), using half the measured flour on board. Return flour and chopped suet to bowl.

Add salt and baking powder. Mix well, using a knife. Add sufficient cold water to make an elastic dough.

Flour board lightly and turn out pastry. Handle quickly and lightly. Roll out, to and fro, and use as required.

SHORT CRUST PASTRY.

Aim. To make light, crisp and well-cooked.

4 ozs. flour.
$1\frac{1}{2}$ to 2 ozs. butter, dripping or margarine and lard.
$\frac{1}{4}$ teaspoonful salt.
Cold water.

Method.

Heat oven. Measure flour into bowl. Add salt. Measure fat and add to flour in bowl. Chop fat with a knife, then rub into flour using the fingertips for coolness. The mixture should be like breadcrumbs. Add sufficient cold water to make a stiff paste. Turn pastry on to floured board. Knead lightly, roll out, to and fro, and use as required.

NOTE. Half lard and half margarine may be used.

ROUGH PUFF PASTRY.

Aim. To make light, flaky and well-cooked.

4 ozs. flour.   3 ozs. butter, dripping or lard and margarine.
$\frac{1}{4}$ teaspoonful salt.
Cold water.

Method.

Heat oven. Measure flour into bowl. Add salt. Measure fat into bowl and cut in fairly large pieces. Add sufficient water to make an elastic dough. Turn on to floured board, press lightly into an oblong shape, keeping the corners square. Roll lightly to $\frac{1}{8}$th inch. Fold up $\frac{1}{3}$rd and down $\frac{1}{3}$rd, like an envelope. Press edges lightly with rolling-pin to seal up air. Turn half-way round. Repeat this rolling and folding process 3 times. Roll out to shape required.

NOTE. Half lard and half margarine may be used.

FLAKY PASTRY.

Aim. To make light, flaky and well-cooked.

4 ozs. flour.   3 ozs. butter, dripping, lard or margarine.
¼ teaspoonful salt.
lemon juice.
cold water.

Method.
Heat oven.
Measure flour into bowl, add salt.
Divide fat into four pieces. Rub one piece into flour, till like bread-crumbs. Add water and squeeze of lemon juice and mix to a stiff paste, using a knife.
Turn on to a floured board and roll into an oblong ⅛th inch thick.
Place one quarter of fat, in pats, over ⅔rds of pastry. Fold in three, folding the plain part over the fat, first of all. Seal edges lightly with the rolling-pin to enclose air.
Half turn and roll into an oblong. Repeat twice more till all the fat is used up. Roll out to shape required.

PUDDINGS.

MILK PUDDINGS.

Proportions.		Using egg:—	
	1 pint milk.		1 pint milk.
	2 ozs. grain.		1½ ozs. grain.
	1 oz. sugar.		1 oz. sugar.
	Pinch salt.		Pinch salt.

There are 3 types of milk puddings:—
1. **Powders,** e.g., cornflour, custard powder and arrowroot.
   For these, the powder is blended with part of the measured milk.
2. **Fine grains,** e.g., semolina, farola and ground rice.
   For these, the grain is sprinkled into the measured milk.
3. **Coarse grains,** e.g., rice, tapioca.
   For these, all the ingredients are placed together in pie-dish.

BAKED RICE PUDDING.

Recipe.

½ pint milk.   Pinch salt.
1 oz. rice.   ¼ oz. butter.
½ oz. sugar.

Heat oven, grease pie-dish and wash rice through a strainer. Place in pie-dish with sugar and salt. Cover with milk, add butter. Bake in a slow oven 1½ hours till creamy and grains soft. Stir pudding when half cooked.
NOTE. Tapioca pudding is made in the same way.

SEMOLINA PUDDING.

Recipe. ½ pint milk.
1 oz. semolina.
½ oz. sugar.
Pinch salt.

Method. Grease
pie-dish and rinse pan
in cold water. Warm milk
in pan and sprinkle in
semolina, stirring all the
time to prevent lumps.
Bring to the boil and cook for 5
minutes, continuing to stir with
wooden spoon. Add sugar and salt
and pour into pie-dish. Brown under
the grill.

NOTE. If using egg, allow
pudding to cool slightly, beat
in egg and pour all into pie-
dish. Farola and ground rice
puddings are cooked in the
same way.

CUSTARD MOULD.

Recipe. ½ pint milk.
1 oz. custard powder.
½ oz. sugar.
Pinch salt.

Method. Fill mould with
cold water. Rinse pan with
cold water, measure milk, and
pour half of the milk into pan and
warm. Put remainder of milk into bowl,
add custard powder and blend till smooth
with a wooden spoon. Pour warmed milk
over, still stirring to prevent lumps. Return
all to pan and boil up, stirring all the time. Boil
for 5 minutes. Add sugar and salt and pour into
mould. When cold, turn mould into a crystal dish.
NOTE. Cornflour and arrowroot puddings are made in
the same way.

48

STEAMED CUSTARD.

Aim. To have a smooth velvety texture when cooked.

Recipe. ¼ pint milk.
1 egg.
1 teaspoonful sugar.
Pinch salt.

Method.
Prepare pan,
bowl and paper
for steaming. Warm
the milk, beat egg
slightly to mix yolk and
white. Stir into milk. Add
sugar and salt. Pour into
greased bowl and steam **very
gently** for ½ hour till set and
smooth.
Serve daintily on hot dish. This
dish is suitable for invalids.

BAKED CUSTARD. Use double the
amount of milk in recipe. Heat oven.
Grease pie-dish. Prepare mixture as above
and pour into pie-dish. Place pie-dish on a
baking-tin and bake in a **slow** oven ½ hour till
set and brown.

MACARONI PUDDING.

Recipe.
1 oz. macaroni.
½ oz. sugar.
Pinch salt.
½ pint milk.
¼ oz. butter.

Method. Heat oven. Grease pie-dish. Measure macaroni, sugar, salt and milk into pie-dish.
Place pat of butter on top. Bake in a slow oven for 1½ hours. Stir with a fork when half-cooked.
The pudding should be creamy and a pale brown when ready.

CURDS.

Recipe.
1 pint milk.
2 teaspoonfuls rennet.
1 oz. sugar.

Method. Rinse pan in cold water. Measure milk into pan, add sugar and warm till blood
heat. Stir in rennet from a teaspoon. Pour into crystal dish and leave 2 or 3 hours to set.

D

FRUIT.

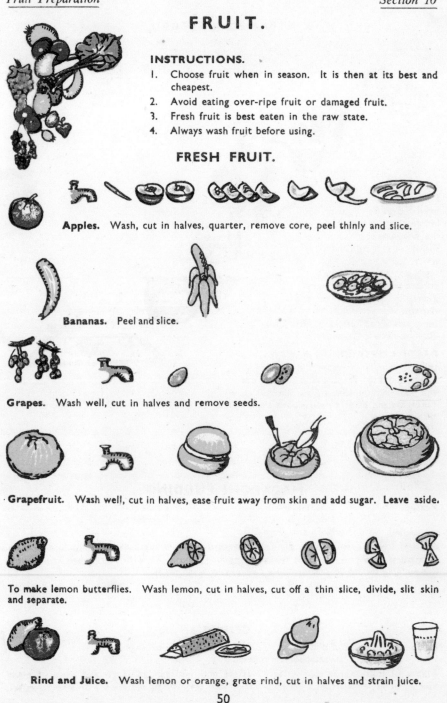

INSTRUCTIONS.

1. Choose fruit when in season. It is then at its best and cheapest.
2. Avoid eating over-ripe fruit or damaged fruit.
3. Fresh fruit is best eaten in the raw state.
4. Always wash fruit before using.

FRESH FRUIT.

Apples. Wash, cut in halves, quarter, remove core, peel thinly and slice.

Bananas. Peel and slice.

Grapes. Wash well, cut in halves and remove seeds.

Grapefruit. Wash well, cut in halves, ease fruit away from skin and add sugar. **Leave** aside.

To make lemon butterflies. Wash lemon, cut in halves, cut off a thin slice, divide, slit skin and separate.

Rind and Juice. Wash lemon or orange, grate rind, cut in halves and strain juice.

Gooseberries. Wash well, top and tail with scissors.

Strawberries. Remove husks and any over-ripe fruit.

Raspberries. Remove husks and any over-ripe fruit.

Plums, Cherries. Wash well, remove stalks and pick over.

Rhubarb. Trim leaves and white ends, wash well and cut in small pieces.

DRIED FRUIT.

Prunes, Apricots, Apple Rings. Wash well and steep overnight in cold water.

Figs. Remove stalks, wash well and steep overnight in cold water.

Raisins, Sultanas, Currants. Place in corner of dish-towel, sprinkle with flour, gather up corner of towel, rub hard, then pick out fruit, removing any stalks.

51

STEWED FRESH FRUIT.

Apples.
Rhubarb.
Gooseberries.
Plums, Etc.

INSTRUCTIONS.

Prepare fruit as shown on (page 50).
Place sugar and water in pan, bring to the boil and boil for 5 minutes till syrupy. Add fruit and stew slowly till tender (see stewing page 13).

Time for stewing. 15 to 20 minutes.

PROPORTIONS.
1 lb. fresh fruit.
4 ozs. sugar.
1 gill water.

DRIED FRUIT.

Prunes.
Apricots.
Figs.
Apple Rings.

INSTRUCTIONS.

Place fruit and water in pan and stew slowly till tender. Add sugar 10 minutes before serving.

Time for stewing.
½ to ¾ hour.

PROPORTIONS.
1 lb. dried fruit.
2 ozs. sugar.
½ pint water.

PUDDINGS, HOT AND COLD.

STEAMED PUDDINGS.

For all steamed puddings, first prepare pan, bowl and paper to cover (see steaming page 12).

Aim. To serve light, spongy and well-cooked.

Causes of heavy, sodden puddings.

1. Careless measuring.
2. Slowness in getting pudding on to cook after adding liquid.
3. Allowing water in the steamer to go off the boil.
4. Insufficient cooking.

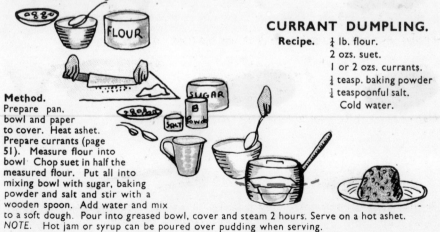

CURRANT DUMPLING.

Recipe. ¼ lb. flour.
2 ozs. suet.
1 or 2 ozs. currants.
¼ teasp. baking powder
¼ teaspoonful salt.
Cold water.

Method.

Prepare pan, bowl and paper to cover. Heat ashet. Prepare currants (page 51). Measure flour into bowl. Chop suet in half the measured flour. Put all into mixing bowl with sugar, baking powder and salt and stir with a wooden spoon. Add water and mix to a soft dough. Pour into greased bowl, cover and steam 2 hours. Serve on a hot ashet.

NOTE. Hot jam or syrup can be poured over pudding when serving.

STEAMED GINGER PUDDING.

Recipe.　4 ozs. flour.
2 ozs. suet.
¼ teaspoon baking soda.
¼ teaspoon ground
ginger.
½ oz. sugar.
Pinch salt.
1 dessertspoon syrup.
Milk to mix.

NOTE. Chopped dates
or figs may be added
with dry ingre-
dients.

Method.
Prepare pan,
bowl and paper
for steaming.
Heat ashet, measure
flour into bowl. Chop suet and
add to flour. Place plate over bowl
and measure dry ingredients on to
plate. Check ingredients on plate then
add to bowl. Stir with a wooden spoon.
Mix syrup with a little milk and beat into
mixture, adding more milk if necessary till
mixture is of a dropping consistency.
Pour into a greased bowl, cover and steam
2 hours. Serve on a hot ashet.

PLUM PUDDING.

Recipe.
3 ozs. raisins
3 ozs. currants.
1 lemon.
4 ozs. breadcrumbs.
2 ozs. mixed peel.
¼ lb. suet.
½ lb. flour.
2 ozs. brown sugar.
½ teaspoon mixed spice
¼ teaspoon salt. 1 egg.
¾ teaspoon baking soda. Milk.
2 tablespoons treacle.

Method.
Heat water
in pan. Grease bowl
and paper (steaming
page) clean fruit.
Stone raisins and cut in
halves. Wash lemon and
grate rind. Grate bread.
Chop peel. Measure flour into
large bowl and use some of the flour
on board when chopping suet. Chop
suet till like breadcrumbs. Measure
spices, soda, salt and sugar on to plate.
Add to flour. Add fruit and peel and stir
well with a wooden spoon. Beat eggs,
squeeze lemon juice and add to bowl with
dry ingredients.　　Add egg, milk and
treacle. Mix to a dropping consistency,
adding more milk if necessary. Pour
into greased bowl, cover with paper and
steam for 4 hours. Heat ashet and serve
pudding.

BAKED APPLE.

I apple, sugar, syrup,
honey, dates, etc.

Method. Heat oven. Heat ashet. Wash apple. Remove core with apple corer or with handle of teaspoon. Place apple on baking tin and fill centre with sugar or honey, etc. Bake in a moderate oven for 20 to 30 minutes. Apple should be soft but not broken. Serve on hot ashet.

STEAMED APPLE DUMPLING.

4 ozs. suet crust pastry.
2 apples. $1\frac{1}{2}$ to 2 ozs. sugar.
2 teaspoons water.

Method.
Prepare pan, bowl and paper to cover. Prepare apples (page 50). Cut in thin slices. Prepare pastry. Cut off piece for lid.
Roll pastry into a round $\frac{1}{8}$th inch thick. Line bowl with pastry, fill centre with half the fruit, add sugar and water, then the rest of the fruit. Damp edges of pastry. Roll out lid to fit top and cover, press edges together lightly. Cover with paper and steam $1\frac{1}{2}$ to 2 hours. Serve on hot ashet.
NOTE. 1 or 2 cloves may be used to flavour.

BAKED JAM ROLY-POLY.

$\frac{1}{4}$ lb. suet crust pastry.
Jam.

Method.
Heat oven. Heat ashet. Prepare pastry (page 45). Roll pastry into an oblong $\frac{1}{8}$th inch thick, spread with jam to within an inch from edge. Roll up, place on greased baking tin and bake in a fairly hot oven $\frac{1}{2}$ hour. Serve on hot ashet.

STEAMED JAM LAYER PUDDING.

$\frac{1}{4}$ lb. suet crust pastry.
Jam.

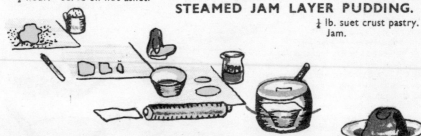

Method. Prepare pan, bowl and paper to cover.
Heat ashet, prepare pastry, divide into 3 various-sized pieces. Roll out to $\frac{1}{8}$th inch thick. Place a little jam in bottom of bowl. Place smallest round on jam. Continue in this way, making layers of jam and pastry. Finish with layer of pastry. Cover with paper and steam $1\frac{1}{2}$ hours. Turn on to ashet and serve hot.

BAKED PUDDINGS.
BAKED BREAD AND BUTTER PUDDING.

Recipe. 2 slices bread.
Butter.
2 ozs. sultanas.
½ egg.
1½ teacups milk.
Pinch salt.
½ oz. sugar.

Method.
Heat oven.
Grease pie-dish.
Prepare sultanas
(page 51)
Butter bread, cut in
neat squares and put
half in pie-dish.
Sprinkle sultanas over
and add rest of bread.
Beat egg and sugar, add milk
and salt and pour over bread.
Leave to soak for 15 minutes.
Bake in a moderate oven for ¾ hour
till crisp on top, golden-brown and set.
Serve pie-dish on a cold ashet.

BAKED CHOCOLATE PUDDING.

Recipe.   ¼ lb. flour.   ½ teaspoon baking powder.
1½ ozs. butter.   ½ egg.
1½ ozs. sugar.   Milk.
2 ozs. chocolate or cocoa.

VARIETIES.

Canary Pudding—add grated rind of 1 lemon.

Orange Pudding—add grated rind of 1 orange.

Raisin Pudding—add 2 ozs. prepared raisins.

Ginger Pudding—add 2 ozs. prepared ginger or ¼ teaspoon ground ginger.

Note. These puddings may be steamed.

Method. Heat oven. Grease pie-dish. Cream butter and sugar with a wooden spoon·
Mix flour and cocoa and add alternately with egg. Add baking powder with the last spoonful
of flour. Add milk till mixture is of a dropping consistency. Spread in pie-dish and bake in a
moderate oven till well-risen and firm on top—¾ hour.

APPLE CHARLOTTE.

Recipe.   3 cooked apples.   2 ozs. breadcrumbs.
Grated rind of 1 lemon.   1 oz. butter.
2 ozs. sugar.

Method. Heat oven. Grease pie-dish. Stew apples till tender. Mix breadcrumbs, sugar
and lemon rind together in bowl and place alternate layers of mixture and apples in pie-dish,
finishing with breadcrumbs. Dot over top with small pats of butter. **Bake in a moderate**
oven for 30 minutes. Serve pie-dish on cold ashet.

EVE'S PUDDING.

Recipe.   2 ozs. butter.
                2 ozs. sugar.
                I egg.
                3 ozs. flour.
                ½ teaspoon baking powder
                A little milk.

STEW { I lb. apples.
        { 2 ozs. sugar.

Method.
Heat oven.
Grease pie-dish.
Stew apples till
tender and
and spread
in bottom of
pie-dish.
Cream butter and
sugar with a wooden
spoon.
Beat egg. Add egg
and flour alternately.
Measure baking powder
and add with the last spoonful
of flour. Add milk if necessary.
Spread mixture over apples and bake
in a moderate oven till sponge is well-
cooked and risen—about ¾ hour.
Serve pie-dish on a cold ashet.

QUEEN OF PUDDINGS.

Recipe.   ½ pint milk.
                I oz. butter.
                I teacup breadcrumbs.
                grated rind of I lemon.
                I oz. sugar.
                2 eggs.
                Jam.

Method.
Heat oven.
Grease pie-dish.
Crumble bread
into bowl and add
sugar.
Warm milk and butter
and pour over bread.
Soak 10 minutes.
Separate yolks and whites,
having whites on a plate.
Add yolk to mixture in bowl.
Mix all ingredients together
and pour into pie-dish.
Bake in a moderate oven for ½ hour.
Remove from oven and spread top with jam.
Beat whites stiffly, fold in 4 ozs. castor sugar,
pile meringue on top of pudding. Bake
slowly till meringue is pale brown.

RHUBARB CRISPIE.

Recipe.   ¼ lb. flour.   1 oz. sugar.
                     2 ozs. butter.   Pinch salt.
Stew.   3 or 4 stalks rhubarb.   1½ to 2 ozs. sugar.

Method.   Stew rhubarb with sugar and place in pie-dish.   Rub fat into flour with the finger-tips till like fine breadcrumbs.   Add sugar and salt and mix.

Sprinkle roughly over rhubarb in pie-dish.   Place pie-dish on baking-tin and bake ¾ hour till crisp on top and cooked.   Serve pie-dish on cold ashet.

Note.   Stewed apples or tinned fruit may be used instead of rhubarb.

BAKED APPLE BALL.

Recipe. 1 apple.
2 ozs. short crust pastry.
sugar.   1 clove.

Method.
Heat oven and ashet.
Prepare apple. Wash and peel thinly and remove core with an apple corer or with handle of a teaspoon.
Prepare short crust pastry (page 46). Roll pastry into a circle ⅛th inch thick, large enough to enfold apple. Lay apple on centre of pastry and work pastry up the sides of apple leaving a hole on top.
Fill hole with sugar, syrup, honey or dates.
Damp edges of pastry and work together till apple is covered. Place a clove on top to represent a stalk. Place apple on baking-tin.
Bake in a fairly hot oven 20 to 30 minutes.
Lift off tin with a fish slice and lay carefully on hot ashet.   Serve hot.

Method.
Heat oven.
Choose a fire-proof plate of suitable size.
Prepare pastry (page 46).
Roll out to ⅛th inch thick, a size larger than plate.
Cut off an edge all round. Damp rim of plate and lay edge round.
Damp edge and lay pastry on to cover plate.
Trim off edges with knife.
Spread tart with jam.
Roll out scraps and cut into lengths, twist and lay in pattern to decorate tart.
Bake in a fairly hot oven for 20 to 25 minutes

OPEN JAM TART.
Recipe.
4 ozs. short crust pastry,
Jam.

SYRUP TART FILLING.
Grated rind and juice of 1 lemon.
6 tablespoons breadcrumbs.
4 tablespoons syrup.

Custard Filling.
1 gill custard.
(page 44)

SPICED FRUIT TART.
(Covered Tart).

Recipe.   8 ozs. short crust pastry.
Filling   I apple.
          ¼ lb. dates.
          2 ozs. sugar.
          ½ teaspoon cinnamon.
          A little water.

Method.
Prepare apple
and stew till tender
with dates, sugar,
cinnamon and water.
Remove stones and leave
on plate to cool. Heat oven.
Prepare pastry (page 46). Divide
pastry in two and roll each part into
a round ⅛th inch thick to fit shallow
sandwich tin or fireproof plate.
Line plate with first round, prick with
fork and spread with filling.
Damp edges and cover with second round.
Press edges lightly together and mark with fork.
Place on baking-tin and bake in a fairly hot oven
20 to 25 minutes.
NOTE.   If liked a small teaspoonful cinnamon
      may be added to the pastry.

APPLE TART

¼ lb. short crust pastry.
2 cooking apples.
3 tablespoons sugar.
I tablespoon cold
                    water.

Heat oven.
Prepare filling.
Wipe, quarter, core
and peel apple. Cut in
slices. Half-fill pie dish with
apple, sprinkle with sugar and
put remaining slices on top. Add
water.   Prepare short crust pastry (page
46). Flour board and roll out pastry to ⅛th inch
thickness (size larger than pie-dish). Cut a strip all round
the pastry to fit rim of pie-dish. Damp rim and lay strip on.
Roll pastry to fit top exactly.   Damp strip and lay top of pastry
on pie-dish.   Press edges together very lightly. Mark edge vertically
with a fork or handle of a teaspoon.   Place on baking-tin and bake in a fairly hot oven 25 to
30 minutes till pastry is well baked, crisp and golden-brown.   Take out of oven and make 2
slits, one at each end to allow steam to escape.   Serve on an ashet.

CHRISTMAS PIES.

Method.
Heat oven. Prepare pastry (page 46). Roll out to ⅛th inch thick. Cut out an equal number of shapes with two cutters of different sizes. Lay a teaspoonful of mincemeat on smaller rounds. Damp edges. Lay larger rounds on top and press edges lightly. Make two slits in top of each pie. Flake edges horizontally with knife and place on baking tin. Brush tops with egg and bake in a fairly hot oven about 20 minutes till well-risen and brown. Dust with sugar and serve hot.

Recipe. 4 ozs. rough puff pastry. mincemeat.

egg to brush. sugar.

APPLE IN BATTER.

Recipe.   I or 2 apples.   ½ pint batter.
Method. Prepare batter (page 92) and lay aside. Heat oven. Grease pie-dish. Prepare apples, slice thinly and arrange in pie-dish. Pour over enough batter to almost cover apples. Bake 20 minutes in a hot oven till well-risen and spongy. Serve hot.

APPLE FRITTERS. (See Deep Frying).

Recipe   I or 2 apples.   ½ pint batter.   Sugar.
Method. Prepare batter (page 92) and lay aside. Heat fat in pan, heat ashet. Have draining paper ready on tin, also dish-paper. Slice apples thinly, dip in batter and fry in smoking hot fat. Lift out with draining spoon when golden-brown, drain, toss in sugar and serve immediately on hot ashet with dish paper.

DINNER PANCAKES.

½ pint batter.
lemon juice.
sugar.
lard to fry.

Method.
Prepare batter (page 92) and lay aside. Heat ashet. Lay sugared paper on board.
Cut lemon in two.
Make lemon butterflies (page 50). Have knife ready, also dish-paper for ashet.
Pour batter into small jug or cup.
Melt ¼ oz. lard in frying pan. When faintly smoking, pour in enough batter to cover bottom of pan. Cook on one side till brown, loosen edges with knife, shake pan then toss pancake or turn with knife. Cook second side.
Turn on to sugared paper, sprinkle with lemon juice, roll up and serve on hot ashet with dish-paper.
Repeat process, greasing pan each time.
NOTE. Hot jam may be used as a filling.

COLD SWEETS. SEMOLINA SNOW.

1 lemon rind.
   (and juice).
1 pint water.
2 ozs. semolina.
3 ozs. sugar.

Method.
Wash lemon.
Grate rind and
add to water in pan
Bring to the boil, re-
move from heat and
sprinkle in semolina, stirring
with a wooden spoon
Cook till grains are clear, about
10 minutes. Add sugar. Cut lemon
and squeeze juice. Add juice to pan,
stir and leave aside to cool in bowl.
Cover bowl with plate, when cool, beat
till white and frothy, using a whisk.
Serve daintily in crystal dish.
NOTE. Stewed rhubarb or plums
(stewed and stoned) may be used instead of lemon.

APPLE SNOW.

Recipe. 1 lb. apples.
4 ozs. sugar.
1 tablespoon water.
½ pint packet lemon jelly.
¼ pint boiling water.
¼ pint cream.
Cherries.

Method.
Stew apples
till tender.
Pour into bowl
and beat till
smooth. Leave
aside to cool.
Dissolve, cut-up
jelly with boiling
water, stir well and
leave aside to cool.
When jelly shows signs of setting,
add apple pulp and beat with a
whisk till light and spongy.
When beginning to set, pile up neatly
in glasses.
Decorate top with whipped cream and
finish with a cherry.

SUMMER PUDDING.

Recipe. I lb. raspberries, red currants, or rhubarb.
4 ozs. sugar.
I tablespoon water.
Slices of bread or sponge cake.

Method.
Stew fruit with sugar and water.
Choose a medium-sized bowl and fit a round of bread in bottom of bowl, then cut rest of bread in neat shapes to line sides of bowl, also a larger round to fit top of bowl.
Fill bowl to top with stewed fruit and place large round of bread on top.
Cover bowl with a plate to fit exactly and place weight on top.
Leave till next day and turn on to serving dish.
Serve with custard sauce (page 44).

TRIFLE.

Recipe
Dry sponge cakes.
Jam.
Tin fruit salad.
$\frac{1}{2}$ pint custard.
I gill cream.
I tablespoon castor sugar.
Few drops of vanilla essence.

Method.
Cut sponge cakes and spread with jam.
Arrange neatly in suitable dish and cover with a layer of fruit, e.g., pineapple cubes or sliced peaches,
Pour over enough fruit syrup to soak sponge.
Make custard (page 48) pour over fruit and leave until cold.
Whip up tinned or double cream, flavour with vanilla and stir in castor sugar.
Spread over trifle and decorate top with cherries, angelica and ratafia biscuits.

FRUIT SALAD.

Recipe.   2 eating apples.
2 bananas.
¼ lb. grapes.
1 lemon.
1 tin fruit salad.
1 oz. sugar.
¼ pint water.

Method.
Make a syrup
by boiling the
water, sugar, lemon
rind and the juice
from the fruit salad for
10 minutes.
Add lemon juice and cool.
Cut grapes in halves and
remove seeds (page 50).
Chop apples and slice
bananas.
Arrange in a crystal dish.
Pour syrup over and leave
aside till required.

JELLIES.

A jelly should be of a trembling
   consistency when served.
Preparation of Mould.
Rinse mould with boiling water then fill with
cold water and leave ready for use.
Always wash and dry moulds thoroughly after
use.

LEMON SPONGE

     (without eggs)
1 pint packet
         lemon jelly.
¼ pint boiling water.
½ pint cold water.
juice of 1 orange
        or lemon·

Method.
Prepare mould. Pour
¼ pint boiling water over
cut-up jelly in a large bowl.
Stir till jelly is dissolved. Add
½ pint cold water and strained
lemon juice. Cover and leave till
jelly shows signs of setting. Whisk
in a cool place till jelly is spongy. Pour
into mould and leave to set. Turn into
crystal dish.
NOTE. Fruit may be added just before
jelly is poured into mould.

TO TURN OUT A JELLY.

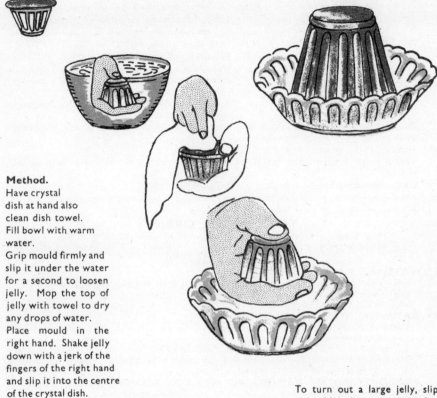

Method.
Have crystal
dish at hand also
clean dish towel.
Fill bowl with warm
water.
Grip mould firmly and
slip it under the water
for a second to loosen
jelly. Mop the top of
jelly with towel to dry
any drops of water.
Place mould in the
right hand. Shake jelly
down with a jerk of the
fingers of the right hand
and slip it into the centre
of the crystal dish.

To turn out a large jelly, slip
mould under warm water for
a second and dry top. Place
large glass dish upside
down over jelly, hold
firmly, turn glass dish
right side up and
shake jelly down
carefully.

MILK JELLY.

Recipe. $1\frac{1}{4}$ ozs. gelatine.   2 or 3 strips of lemon rind.
             3 tablespoons water.   2 ozs. sugar.
             $1\frac{1}{2}$ pints milk.

Method. Prepare mould. Wash lemon and cut off a thin rind. Place rind in pan with milk
and sugar and warm gently for 10 minutes. Dissolve gelatine in a small pan with water over a
gentle heat. When milk is cool, stir in dissolved gelatine and stir quickly to prevent gelatine
setting before being mixed. Strain into mould and leave to set. Serve in a crystal dish.

BAKING FOR TEA.

Aim. To serve light, well-cooked, appetizing dainties.
1. Collect all utensils, etc. before beginning.
2. Lay out foodstuffs required.
3. Heat oven, girdle, etc.
4. Prepare tins first.
5. Measure accurately. If there are several ingredients in recipe, measure them on to a plate and check carefully.
6. Air the flour by using a sieve or by sprinkling it into mixing bowl.
7. After adding the liquid to a raising-agent, work quickly so that the rising takes place in the oven (*exception*—when using yeast).
8. Handle as little as possible and as lightly as possible.
9. Where butter is mentioned, margarine, or lard and margarine, or nutter may be used instead.
10 Scrape out mixing-bowl thoroughly.
11. Attend to oven or girdle but do not open oven door more than is necessary.
12. Put everything away tidily when finished baking.

TO TEST AN OVEN.

Hot Oven. White paper should brown in $1\frac{1}{2}$ minutes.
Moderate Oven. ,,   ,,   ,,   ,,   ,, 2 minutes.

RAISING AGENTS.

A. **NATURAL RAISING AGENTS.**
AIR—As in batter page 92, also included in airing flour and working lightly.
EGG—when beaten holds air.
FAT—when creamed with sugar holds air.

B. **ARTIFICIAL RAISING AGENTS.**
Carbon Dioxide, produced by:—
1. YEAST—when mixed with sugar.
2. BAKING SODA (alkali) and CREAM OF TARTAR (acid)—when milk is added.
3. BAKING POWDER—(made up of 4 ozs. cream of tartar, 2 ozs. baking soda, 6 ozs. rice flour)—when milk is added.

PROPORTIONS OF RAISING AGENTS FOR SCONES, BUNS, ETC.

To I lb. flour.	To I lb. flour.
I teaspoon baking soda.	I teaspoon baking soda.
I teaspoon cream of tartar.	2 teaspoons cream of tartar.
Sour milk or buttermilk.	Sweet milk.

HOW TO KNEAD DOUGH.

Dredge centre of board lightly with flour and rub in with the fingertips to form a skin. Turn out dough, leaving bowl clean.	Toss dough lightly from one hand to another then knead by pulling dough from edges into centre while turning dough round with the left hand.	When free from cracks, turn dough upside down. Flour rolling-pin lightly and rub in flour.	Roll lightly to desired thickness with short, sharp strokes, rolling forward and backward. Do not roll too much. Work quickly.

64

WHITE BREAD.

Recipe.   3½ lbs. flour.
                3½ teaspoons salt.
                1 oz. yeast.
                1 teaspoon sugar
                1½ pints tepid water.

Method.
Mix flour and
salt in bowl. Mix
yeast and sugar to-
gether with wooden
spoon. Add tepid water.
Make a well in centre of flour,
add liquid and mix to an elastic
consistency with the hands. Score
across the top to prevent a skin
forming and place bowl, covered
with clean towel, in a warm place for
1 hour till twice the size (rising).
Grease tins and keep them warm.
Pull and knead the dough firmly to even
up the gas, cut in four pieces and press down
into loaf tins and leave again in a warm place
to rise a little (proving). Bake in a hot oven to
start with, then a moderate heat for about 40
to 60 minutes, according to size.
When ready, the bread should sound hollow
when tapped underneath.

BROWN BREAD.

Recipe.   3 lbs. wheaten meal.   2 ozs. lard.
                  ½ lb. white flour.   1 oz. yeast.
                  3 teaspoons salt.   1 teaspoon sugar.
                  1½ pints tepid water.

Method. Mix wheaten meal and white flour. Add salt and keep warm. Rub fat into flour.
Mix yeast and sugar together, then add tepid water. Add to flour and proceed as for white
bread. Bake in greased loaf tins. Test for hollowness by tapping loaf underneath when
baked.

BAKING POWDER ROLLS.

Recipe.
     ½ lb. flour.
     1 oz. butter or
        lard.
     ½ teaspoon salt.
     1 teaspoon baking
        powder.
     1 gill milk.
     Egg to brush.

Method.
Heat oven.
Grease or flour
baking-tin.
Rub fat into flour.
Add dry ingredients
and mix to an elastic
dough. Knead and shape
into twists and rings.
Brush with egg or milk
and bake in a moderate
oven for 10 to 15 minutes
till light and well cooked.
Cool on a wire tray.

E

OVEN SCONES.

Scones—Aim. To have light, spongy and well risen scones.

Recipe.
¼ lb. flour.
1 oz. butter.
¼ teaspoon salt.
¼ teaspoon baking
                    soda.
¼ teaspoon Cream of
                    Tartar.
½ oz. sugar.
Sour milk.
    egg to brush.

Method.
Heat oven. Grease
or flour baking-tin.
Rub fat into flour.
Add dry ingredients,
crushing out lumps in
baking soda and salt. Add
sour milk and mix to a soft
dough.
Flour board lightly, knead dough and roll
to ½-inch thickness. Divide in four, place on
baking-tin in a circle and bake in a fairly hot
oven 8 to 10 minutes.
Cool on a wire tray. When quite cold serve
on a plate with a d'oyley.
   NOTE. WHEATEN SCONES—Same recipe,
using half wheaten meal and half flour.
SULTANA SCONES—Add 1 oz. fruit to ¼ lb. flour.

GIRDLE SCONES.

Care of the girdle.
1. Rub over carefully before using.
2. Heat girdle very slowly. Turn occasionally.
3. Test by patting quickly with the hand or by sprinkling lightly with
   flour which should turn golden-brown.
4. Do not wash girdle. Scrape if necessary and rub over with soft
   paper.

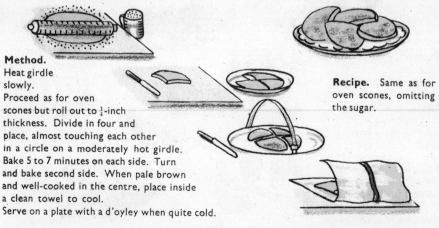

Method.
Heat girdle
slowly.
Proceed as for oven
scones but roll out to ¼-inch
thickness. Divide in four and
place, almost touching each other
in a circle on a moderately hot girdle.
Bake 5 to 7 minutes on each side. Turn
and bake second side. When pale brown
and well-cooked in the centre, place inside
a clean towel to cool.
Serve on a plate with a d'oyley when quite cold.

Recipe. Same as for
oven scones, omitting
the sugar.

POTATO SCONES.

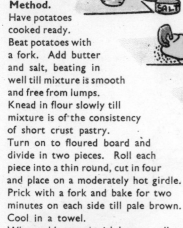

Method.
Have potatoes
cooked ready.
Beat potatoes with
a fork. Add butter
and salt, beating in
well till mixture is smooth
and free from lumps.
Knead in flour slowly till
mixture is of the consistency
of short crust pastry.
Turn on to floured board and
divide in two pieces. Roll each
piece into a thin round, cut in four
and place on a moderately hot girdle.
Prick with a fork and bake for two
minutes on each side till pale brown.
Cool in a towel.
When cold, spread with butter, roll up and
serve daintily on plate with d'oyley.

Recipe.
½ lb. cooked potato.
Pinch salt.
½ oz. melted butter.
2 ozs. flour.

DROPPED SCONES.

Recipe.   ½ lb. flour.
½ teaspoon baking soda
½ teaspoon cream of
                    tartar.
½ teaspoon salt.
1 egg.
1 oz. sugar.
Sour milk.

Method.
Heat girdle.
Mix dry ingre-
dients in bowl.
Beat egg and add
with enough sour milk
to make a thick creamy
mixture, using a wooden
spoon.
Test girdle. Heat should be
moderate. Grease girdle with a
piece of suet on a fork and drop
mixture from the point of a dessertspoon. Turn to other side when
bubbles begin to appear and the
skin underneath is a golden-brown
Bake the second side and cool in a towel.
Serve on a plate with d'oyley.

OATCAKES.

Method.
Heat girdle.
Mix oatmeal and
salt together.
Pour in melted fat
and enough hot water to
make a soft mixture.
Rub over board with oatmeal
and turn out mixture. Knead
into a smooth round and roll out
thinly.
Rub oatcakes with oatmeal to whiten
and cut in four with knife. Shake off loose
meal and place carefully on girdle.
Bake till edges begin to curl up. Place on
baking-tin and toast in a moderate oven till
pale brown. Cool on a wire tray.

Recipe.
4 ozs. fine oatmeal.
¼ teaspoon salt.
½ oz. bacon fat or
      melted dripping.
Hot water.

BUNS.
RASPBERRY BUNS.

Method.
Heat oven.
Grease or flour
tin. Rub fat into
flour. Measure dry
ingredients and add.
Beat egg and add with
enough milk to make an
elastic dough. Turn on to a
floured board, divide in two pieces
and shape each piece into four buns.
Place on tin and make a hollow in centre
of each one, drop in a little jam, brush
with egg or milk and bake in a fairly hot oven
10 to 15 minutes. Cool on a wire tray. Serve
on plate with d'oyley.
Rock Buns. Add 2 ozs. currants with dry ingredients, place in rough heaps on tin, using a fork
and spoon. Omit jam.
Coco-nut Buns. Add 2 ozs. dessicated coco-nut.
Omit jam.
Vanilla Buns. Add 1 teaspoon vanilla essence with
egg and milk. Omit jam.

Recipe. 8 ozs. flour.
3 ozs. butter.
2 to 3 ozs. sugar.
1 teasp. baking powder.
¼ teaspoon salt.
1 egg.
      milk.
      Raspberry jam.

DOUGHNUTS.

Method.
Heat fat
slowly.
Prepare tin with
draining paper (page 15
deep frying).
Measure flour into bowl
and rub in fat.
Add dry ingredients, beat
egg and add egg and
enough milk to make an
elastic consistency.
Turn on to floured board
and roll out to ½-inch, cut
out rings with two different
sized cutters.
Have fat slightly smoking.
Fry doughnuts, turning over
with draining spoon, allowing
5 minutes for cooking.
Drain on paper and toss on sugared
paper. Cool on wire tray and serve
on plate with d'oyley when quite cold.

Recipe. ½ lb. flour.
2 ozs. butter.
½ teasp. baking powder
Pinch salt.
1 egg.
Milk.
Castor sugar.
Fat to fry.

SWISS ROLL.

Method.
Heat oven.
Cut white
paper and lay in
bottom of baking-
tin. Grease paper and
sides of tin lightly.
Beat eggs and sugar till
thick and creamy (about
10 minutes).
Mix flour and salt together
and fold into mixture with
a large spoon. Add baking powder
with the last spoonful of flour. Add
enough water to make mixture a thick,
creamy consistency. Pour into tin and
spread quickly. Bake in a fairly hot oven
for 20 minutes. Damp a sheet of white paper and
sprinkle with castor sugar. Have jam ready and a
bread knife. Lay swiss roll upside down on paper. Cut
off edges quickly with knife, spread with jam and roll up
quickly, turning the paper over the roll. Hold roll in position
for a minute, then lift roll on to wire tray and cool.
Serve on plate with d'oyley when quite cold.

Recipe.
3 ozs. castor sugar.
2 eggs.
3 ozs. flour.
½ teaspoon baking
　　　　　　powder.
A little water.

ECCLES CAKES.

Recipe.   Scraps of rough puff pastry.   Currants.   Egg to brush.   Sugar.
Method.   Clean the currants.   Roll scraps to ¼-inch, cut into rounds.   Place 1 teaspoonful currants on each round, gather up edges and press together, turn upside down and roll till currants appear.   Score with knife, lay on tin, brush with egg, sprinkle with sugar and bake in a fairly hot oven till golden-brown and crisp (20 minutes).   Cool on wire tray.

HOW TO LINE A CAKE-TIN.

1. Cut white paper to fit bottom of tin.
2. Measure and cut paper to go all round tin, allowing 3 inches extra, above the height of the tin.   Turn up 1 inch and snip with scissors.
3. Grease paper lightly and fit inside tin.   Grease and fit paper in bottom of tin.

TO TEST A CAKE FOR READINESS.

1. Skewer, inserted in centre of cake, should come out quite free from dough.
2. Cake should feel firm on top.
3. If cake is ready, there should be a space between cake and the sides of the tin.

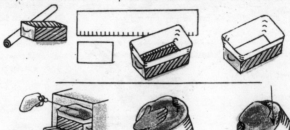

CAKE-MAKING.

INSTRUCTIONS.

Oven. The middle of the oven is best for large cakes.   Allow 20 minutes to heat gas oven.   30 to 40 minutes to heat electric oven.   Sponge sandwiches and small cakes should be fairly near the top of a moderate oven.   For a plain cake have a moderate oven—for a rich cake a slower heat.

Flour. Sieve beforehand.   In making sponges, fold in flour with a turning movement, using a tablespoon.

Fat. Never allow fat to melt when creaming with sugar.

Eggs. Always break eggs separately into a cup, then, if fresh, into a bowl for beating.

Fruit. Prepare as on page 51, removing stalks.

BAKING POWDER. Mix with the last tablespoonful of flour and add.

Tins. When cake is turned out, rub out cake-tin with soft paper.   Do not wash.

PLAIN FRUIT CAKE.

Recipe.   ½ lb. flour.   2 ozs. raisins.
2 ozs. butter.   2 ozs. sultanas.
2 ozs. castor sugar.   1 egg.
½ teasp. baking powder.   ¼ teaspoon salt.
Milk.

Method.

Heat oven.
Grease and flour cake-tin. Measure flour and rub in fat.
Measure dry ingredients.
Prepare fruit and add with dry ingredients. Beat egg and add, with enough milk to make a dropping consistency.
Pour into tin and bake in a moderately hot oven for ¾ hour. Test for readiness.
Cool on a wire tray.

WHITE CAKE.
(Rich)

Method.
Heat oven.
Prepare cake
tin by lining it
with greased paper.
Beat sugar and butter
together with a wooden
spoon until creamy.
Beat eggs till thick. Sieve
flour and salt and add
alternately with egg, beating
well. Add baking powder mixed with
the last spoonful of flour.
Add milk and mix to a dropping consistency. Bake in a moderate oven for
1 hour. Test for readiness. Cool on a wire tray.

Recipe.
$\frac{1}{4}$ lb. butter.
$\frac{1}{4}$ lb. sugar.
2 eggs.
$\frac{1}{2}$ lb. flour.
$\frac{1}{4}$ teaspoon salt.
$\frac{1}{2}$ teaspoon baking
        powder.
Milk

QUEEN CAKES.

2 ozs. butter.   2 ozs. currants.
2 ozs. castor sugar. 2 eggs.
3 ozs. flour.   A little grated lemon
    Pinch salt.   rind.
$\frac{1}{4}$ teaspoon baking powder.

Method.
Brush cake-tins sparingly with
melted lard. Proceed as for a rich cake, by
creaming butter and sugar. Beat egg till thick and work
in alternately with flour, salt, baking powder and lemon rind. Add prepared currants. Mix in
enough milk to make a thick dropping consistency. Place a teaspoonful in each tin and bake
in a fairly hot oven for 20 minutes till spongy and golden-brown. Cool on a wire tray.

WELSH CHEESECAKES.

Method.
Line tins with 4 ozs.
short or rough puff pastry,
rolled out to $\frac{1}{8}$th inch and cut in
rounds to fit patty tins. Put a teaspoonful of jam in each one. Prepare queen cake
mixture as above and drop a spoonful over jam
in each tin. Bake in a fairly hot oven 20 minutes
till pastry is crisp and filling is spongy. Cool on a
wire tray.

SPONGE SANDWICH.

Method.
Heat oven.
Grease and
flour sandwich
tins.
Beat eggs and
sugar for 15 to 20
minutes till thick and creamy
Sieve flour and salt and add
by folding in gently. Add baking
powder mixed with the last spoonful of flour.
Add hot water to make a thick creamy
consistency. Divide mixture between two
tins and bake in a fairly hot oven about 20
minutes till firm and spongy. Turn out carefully with palette knife. Cool on wire tray and
when quite cold spread one with jam or whipped-
up sweetened cream and sandwich together. Dust
with icing sugar. Serve on dish with d'oyley.

Recipe.

3 eggs.
3 ozs. castor sugar.
4 ozs. flour.
½ teaspoon baking powder.
2 tablespoons hot water.
Pinch salt.

GINGERBREAD.

Recipe. ½ lb. flour.
2 ozs. butter.
2 ozs. syrup.
2 ozs. treacle.
1 rounded tablespoon sugar.
1 teaspoon ground ginger.
½ teaspoon baking soda.
1 tablespoon sultanas.
1 egg.
½ gill milk.

Method.
Heat oven.
Grease and
flour cake-tin.
Melt butter, syrup
and treacle together
in small pan.
Measure flour into bowl
and the other dry ingre-
dients on to plate. Add
dry ingredients to bowl and
stir well with a wooden spoon.
Add contents of pan to bowl.
Beat egg in a small bowl or cup,
using a fork, and add to mixture.
Add milk and beat till smooth and of
a soft consistency. Pour into tin and
bake in a moderately hot oven for ¾ to 1
hour till spongy and well-cooked. Test
with a skewer and cool on a tray.

OATMEAL BISCUITS.

Recipe.
2 ozs. flour.
2 ozs. fine oatmeal.
$1\frac{1}{2}$ ozs. butter or lard.
$\frac{1}{2}$ teaspoon baking powder.
I oz. castor sugar.
Pinch salt.
A little milk.

Method.
Heat oven.
Grease tin.
Measure flour
into bowl, add
fat and rub in till
like breadcrumbs.
Measure dry ingredients
on to plate and add. Stir
with wooden spoon. Add
enough milk to make a firm
dough. Rub board with oatmeal,
turn out dough and roll out to $\frac{1}{4}$ inch.
Cut into rounds with cutter, place on
baking-tin and prick with a fork.
Bake in a fairly hot oven for 10 minutes till
crisp. Cool on a wire tray. Serve on a plate with
a d'oyley when quite cold.

ABERNETHY BISCUITS.

Recipe.
$1\frac{1}{2}$ tablespoons sugar.
$\frac{1}{4}$ teacup milk.
$\frac{1}{2}$ lb. flour.
2 ozs. margarine.
2 ozs. lard.
Pinch salt.

Method. Heat oven.
Grease tin. Warm milk
and sugar in small pan and
cool. Measure flour and rub
in lard and margarine till like
breadcrumbs. Add salt. Pour
milk and sugar into mixture and
stir with a knife. Mixture should
be stiff. Roll out on floured board
and cut in rounds. Place on tin and
prick with fork. Bake in a moderate
oven 10 to 15 minutes till pale brown.
Cool on a wire tray.

PARKINS.

Recipe. 2 ozs. flour.
2 ozs. fine oatmeal.
I oz. butter or lard.
$1\frac{1}{2}$ ozs. sugar.
$\frac{1}{2}$ teaspoon baking soda.
$\frac{1}{4}$ teaspoon cinnamon.
$\frac{1}{4}$ teaspoon ground ginger.
$\frac{1}{8}$th teaspoon mixed spice.
I small tablespoon syrup.
Almonds.

Method.
Heat oven.
Grease tin.
Measure flour
and oatmeal and
rub in fat.
Measure spices, soda
and sugar on to plate.
Add to bowl and stir well
with wooden spoon. Add syrup
and beat. Shape into small balls and
place on tin. Flatten slightly with knife
and lay half an almond on top of each biscuit.
(To blanch almonds, bring to the boil in small pan,
remove from heat and slip off brown skins).
Bake biscuits in a moderate oven till crisp, about
15 minutes. Cool on a wire tray.

LEMON BISCUITS.

Recipe.　　　2 ozs. butter.　　　　　　　6 ozs. flour.
2 ozs. castor sugar.　　　　$\frac{1}{4}$ teaspoon baking powder.
Rind of I lemon.　　　　　　A little milk.
$\frac{1}{2}$ egg.

Method. Heat oven. Cream butter and sugar together with a wooden spoon. Grate lemon rind and add with beaten egg. Work in flour and baking powder and mix to a stiff consistency, adding a little milk if necessary. Flour board and roll out to $\frac{1}{4}$-inch. Cut in shapes and place on baking-tin. Prick with a fork and bake till pale-brown in a moderate oven, about 15 minutes. Remove from oven, dip biscuits in castor sugar and cool on a wire tray.

CRUNCHY BISCUITS.

Recipe.　　　$\frac{1}{4}$ lb. flour.　　　　　　　$\frac{1}{2}$ teaspoon baking soda.
$\frac{1}{4}$ lb. flaked meal.　　　　　$\frac{1}{4}$ lb. butter.
$1\frac{1}{2}$ ozs. castor sugar.　　　　I tablespoon syrup.

Method. Heat oven. Grease tin. Warm fat and syrup in pan. Measure flour, flaked meal, sugar and baking soda into bowl, mix together with wooden spoon and stir in fat and syrup. Shape into small balls with the hands and place on tin with a space between each one. Flatten slightly with knife and bake in a moderate oven 10 to 15 minutes till crisp. Leave on tin for 5 minutes till biscuits stiffen, Cool on a wire tray.

74

EMPIRE BISCUITS.

Recipe. 3 ozs. butter.
4 ozs. castor sugar.
½ egg.   8 ozs. flour.
½ teaspoon cinnamon.
¼ teaspoon baking powder.
Pinch salt.
Water icing (page 91).
Cherries.   Jam.

Method.
Heat oven.
Grease tin.
Cream butter
and sugar together
with a wooden spoon.
Beat egg and add with
flour, salt, baking powder
and cinnamon.
Leave for a short time then flour
board and roll out to ¼-inch. Cut
into rounds. Place on baking-tin and
prick with fork. Bake in a moderate oven
for 15 minutes. Cool on a wire tray and when
quite cold sandwich two biscuits together with
jam, ice the tops with water icing (page 91), place
half a cherry on each biscuit and leave to set.
Serve on a plate with a d'oyley.

GYPSY CREAMS.

Recipe. 2 ozs. margarine.   2 ozs. lard.
1 tablespoon grated chocolate.
½ teacup sugar.   1 tablespoon water.
2 cups flaked meal.   1 cup flour.
½ teaspoon baking soda.

Method.
Heat oven.
Grease tin.
Cream fat and
sugar together with
a wooden spoon.
Measure dry ingredients
on to plate and add.
Stir well and mix to a stiff
paste with water. Shape with
the hands into small ovals and
place on baking tin. Flatten
slightly and mark along the top
with the prongs of a fork. Bake
in a moderate oven for 15 mins.
Cool on a wire tray. When cool
sandwich together with chocolate water icing. Serve on a
plate with a d'oyley.

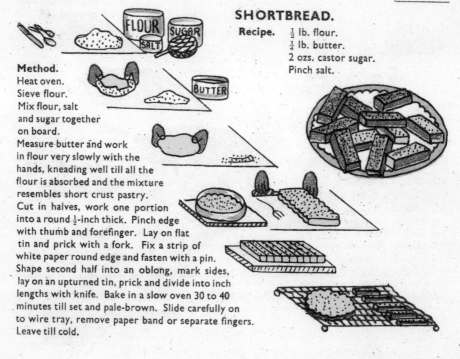

SHORTBREAD.

Recipe. $\frac{1}{2}$ lb. flour.
$\frac{1}{4}$ lb. butter.
2 ozs. castor sugar.
Pinch salt.

Method.
Heat oven.
Sieve flour.
Mix flour, salt
and sugar together
on board.
Measure butter and work
in flour very slowly with the
hands, kneading well till all the
flour is absorbed and the mixture
resembles short crust pastry.
Cut in halves, work one portion
into a round $\frac{1}{2}$-inch thick. Pinch edge
with thumb and forefinger. Lay on flat
tin and prick with a fork. Fix a strip of
white paper round edge and fasten with a pin.
Shape second half into an oblong, mark sides,
lay on an upturned tin, prick and divide into inch
lengths with knife. Bake in a slow oven 30 to 40
minutes till set and pale-brown. Slide carefully on
to wire tray, remove paper band or separate fingers.
Leave till cold.

CHEESE DISHES.

Cheese is very concentrated and it is therefore indigestible if eaten in large pieces. To make it more digestible we can—

    (1) Take it in very small quantities and chew it well.
    (2) Grate it finely.
    (3) Mix it with some starchy food—e.g., potato, bread, etc.
    (4) Season well.

When making up cheese dishes, season well and do not over-cook. Serve hot.

WELSH RAREBIT.

Recipe. ¼ lb. cheese.
Seasoning.
¼ teaspoon mustard.
1 tablespoon milk.
¼ oz. butter.
½ slice toast.

Method.
Heat ashet.
Prepare buttered
toast and keep hot.
Grate cheese. Warm milk and
add cheese, seasoning, mustard and
butter. Stir with a wooden spoon till
smooth, but do not boil. Pour over toast
on ashet. Garnish with a sprig of parsley and serve hot.

MACARONI CHEESE.

Recipe. 3 ozs. macaroni.
Boiling salted water.
2 ozs. cheese.
½ pint white sauce
        (page 42).
    Seasoning.

Method.
Grease piedish. Drop
macaroni into boiling salted
water and boil till tender, about
20 to 30 minutes. Grate cheese. Drain
macaroni water into bowl. Make white
sauce (using half macaroni water and half milk).
Add macaroni, half the cheese and the seasoning. Pour
into pie-dish, sprinkle rest of cheese on top and brown under
the grill. Serve hot.

POTATOES AND CHEESE.

Recipe. 2 ozs. cheese.
4 cooked potatoes.
½ gill milk.
seasoning.
1 oz. butter.

Method.
Heat oven.
Grease pie-dish.
Have potatoes cooked
ready. Grate cheese. Beat
potatoes, add milk, butter, seasoning
and half of the cheese. Mix well together
and arrange neatly in pie-dish. Sprinkle rest of
cheese on top. Heat and brown in the oven.
NOTE. This mixture may be shaped into rissoles, coated and fried.

CHEESE PUDDING.
Recipe.

½ pint milk.   I oz. butter.
3 ozs. cheese.   Seasoning.
3 ozs. breadcrumbs.   I egg.
½ teaspoon mustard.

Method.
Heat oven.
Grease pie-dish.
Grate cheese then bread.
Warm milk and butter and
pour over cheese and breadcrumbs
in bowl, add made-up mustard and seasoning.
Add beaten-up egg and pour into pie-dish.
Bake in a moderate oven 20 to 30 minutes,
till set and brown. Place pie-dish on ashet
and serve hot.

DUTCH CHEESE.

Recipe.   2 slices bread.   ½ oz. butter.
Seasoning.   I oz. cheese.
Fat to fry.

Method.
Heat ashet and prepare
draining paper on tin. Butter one
slice of bread. Grate cheese or slice thinly
and spread over butter. Add seasoning.
Press second slice on top and cut into four
sandwiches. Fry in smoking hot fat on both
sides till golden-brown, drain on paper and serve on hot ashet with dish paper.

POTATO, LEEK AND CHEESE HOT-POT.

Recipe.   I leek.   Salt and pepper.
3 potatoes.   ½ cup milk.
2 ozs. grated cheese.   I oz. butter.

Method. Heat oven. Prepare leeks (page 36) and shred finely. Peel and slice potatoes.
Grate cheese.   Arrange layers of each with salt and pepper in pyrex dish or casserole. Pour
milk over to half-fill dish.   Sprinkle cheese over top and add pats of butter.   Place lid on
and bake in a moderate oven for I hour.

EGG DISHES.

A fresh egg should feel heavy and, if held up to the light, it should be clear with no sign of a black speck. A new-laid egg is more digestible. Eggs are most plentiful and cheaper from Easter till June—this is the time to pickle them.

TO POACH AN EGG.

Heat ashet. Toast ½ slice bread, butter it and keep it hot. Boil water in a shallow pan. Add ¼ teaspoonful salt. Break egg carefully into a cup. Remove pan from heat, stir water in a circular move-ment and slip egg into water. Poach for 2 to 3 minutes till egg is set. Lift out carefully with draining spoon and serve on top of toast. Garnish with a sprig of parsley.

BOILED EGG.

Boil enough water to cover egg, using a small pan. Re-move pan from heat and place egg in carefully. Simmer 3 to 4 minutes according to taste or use an egg-timer.

SCRAMBLED EGG ON TOAST.

1 egg.   ½ slice toast.
1 tablespoon milk.
¼ oz. butter.
Seasoning.

Heat ashet. Prepare buttered toast and keep hot. Beat egg and add milk and seasoning. Melt butter in pan, pour in egg mixture and stir gently with a wooden spoon till thick and creamy. Pile up on top of toast. De-corate with a sprig of par-sley.

FRIED BACON AND EGG.

Recipe.   1 egg.   2 ozs. bacon.

Method. Heat ashet. Cut rind from bacon. Fry bacon slowly in pan till fat is clear and keep hot on ashet. Break egg into cup carefully, slip gently into pan and baste with fat till egg is set. Lift out gently and place on top of bacon. Serve hot.

FRENCH TOAST.

1 slice bread.   Seasoning.
1 egg.   2 tablespoons
Fat to fry.   milk.

Method. Heat ashet. Cut bread in 2 inch squares. Beat egg, add seasoning and milk. Dip bread in egg and fry in hot fat till golden-brown. Serve hot.

NOTE. This dish may be served as a pudding by omitting salt and pepper and sprinkling with sugar before serving.

SAVOURY OMELET.

Recipe. 2 eggs.
2 tablespoons milk.
I oz. butter. Seasoning.

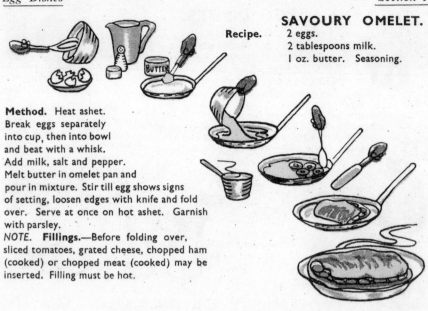

Method. Heat ashet.
Break eggs separately
into cup, then into bowl
and beat with a whisk.
Add milk, salt and pepper.
Melt butter in omelet pan and
pour in mixture. Stir till egg shows signs
of setting, loosen edges with knife and fold
over. Serve at once on hot ashet. Garnish
with parsley.
NOTE. **Fillings.**—Before folding over,
sliced tomatoes, grated cheese, chopped ham
(cooked) or chopped meat (cooked) may be
inserted. Filling must be hot.

EGGS IN WHITE SAUCE.

Recipe.   2 eggs.   Parsley.
I gill white sauce (page 42).

Method. Chop parsley. Boil 2 eggs for 5 minutes, remove shells, cut eggs in halves and
place in pie-dish. Make I gill white sauce (page 42), pour sauce over eggs. Sprinkle with parsley
and serve hot.

HAM AND EGG PIE.

Recipe.   4 ozs. short crust pastry.
Filling.   2 ozs. bacon.   4 tablespoons milk.
2 eggs.   Seasoning.

Method. Heat oven. Line shallow tin with pastry and prick with fork. Chop bacon In small
pieces and lay on pastry. Beat egg and add milk and seasoning. Pour over bacon and bake
in a fairly hot oven, about ½ hour, till golden-brown and set and pastry crisp. Garnish with
parsley and serve hot.

TEA.

I teaspoon tea, ½ pint boiling water sugar and milk to taste. Boil fresh cold water. Heat teapot first, empty water out and put in tea. Pour freshly boiling water over. Infuse 2 or 3 minutes without boiling. Cover with tea-cosy.

COCOA.

I teaspoon cocoa, ½ pint milk or milk and water. Sugar to taste. Blend cocoa with some of the milk. Add to warm milk in the pan and boil. Add sugar. Serve neatly in hot jug.

WHITE COFFEE.

I oz. coffee, ½ pint milk, ⅓ pint water, pinch salt. Heat coffee-pot and strainer. Shake coffee for a second in pan over heat. Add water, milk and salt. Bring to boil and allow to rise three times. Strain into coffee-pot and serve hot. Black coffee is made in the same way, omitting the milk. It is served with cream.

OXO OR BOVRIL.

Follow the directions given and serve neatly with fingers of toast.

LEMONADE.

I lemon, ½ pint boiling water, I oz. sugar. Wash lemon, peel off a very thin rind. Cut lemon in thin slices. Place rind, etc., in jug, add boiling water and sugar, cover and leave to cool. Strain and serve neatly.

EGG FLIP (Invalids).

I egg, ½ gill milk, I teaspoon sugar. Separate yolk and white of egg. Mix yolk and sugar in bowl. Warm the milk, whisk the white of egg till stiff. Pour milk over yolk and stir. Fold in white. Pour into tumbler and serve with a biscuit.

LEMON BARLEY WATER.
(Invalids).

I oz. barley, pinch salt, I pint water, rind and juice of I lemon. Measure barley into pointed strainer. Rinse cold water through strainer then pour boiling water through to scald barley. Peel off lemon rind and put in pan with barley and water. Simmer for 2 hours, strain and add lemon juice and sugar. Serve in a tumbler.

SAGO CREAM (Invalids).

½ pint milk, ½ oz. sago ¼ oz. sugar, pinch salt. I egg.
Rinse pan and warm milk. Sprinkle in sago, stirring well with a wooden spoon. Simmer till sago is clear. Strain and add sugar and salt. Beat egg and mix well. Serve neatly in tumbler.

F

BEEF TEA.

Recipe. ½ lb. gravy beef. Pinch salt.
½ pint water.

I. Quick Method. Wipe meat, remove fat and shred meat finely. Soak in pan with cold water and salt for 15 mins. Stir and press meat against sides of pan while bringing slowly to the boil. Simmer for 10 minutes. Strain, remove any signs of grease and serve with fingers of toast.

2. Slow Method. Prepare meat as above. Place in a jar with cold water and salt and leave to soak for 1 hour—stirring and pressing beef against sides of jar. Place jar (covered with a saucer) in pan of cold water, bring to simmering point and continue cooking for 2 to 3 hours. Finish as above.

FEEDING OF INVALIDS.

INSTRUCTIONS.

1. Carry out the doctor's instructions.
2. Always use best quality ingredients for invalids.
3. Serve dainty portions on a spotless tray and serve punctually.
4. Never serve food left by invalids to other members of the family.
5. Never serve fried food. Methods of cooking should be light and digestible.
6. A good rule when feeding invalids is "little and often."

Liquid Diet. Given when the patient is very weak. When feeding patient, support the head gently by placing left arm behind pillow and raising it slightly. The feeding-cup can then be held in the right hand.

    Lemon Barley Water (page 81).   Lemonade (page 81).   Beef Tea (above).
    Chicken Broth (Strained).   Egg Flip (page 81).   Sago Cream (page 81).
    Bovril and Oxo (page 81).   Milk and Soda Water.

Light Diet. Given when the patient's condition is improving. Food should consist of very small portions. It should be easily eaten and easily digested.

    Chicken Broth or Mutton Broth.   Steamed Whiting (page 26).   Steamed Chicken.
    Scrambled Egg.   Poached Egg.   Boiled Egg (page 79).   Baked Custard.   Steamed Custard
    (page 49).   Curds (page 49).   Milk Jelly, Cocoa, Ovaltine, Horlicks, Toast, Milk.

Convalescent Diet. Given when the patient's strength has improved. This is the stage when the patient's strength must be built up with nourishing food.

    Soups made with stock, Pulse Soups, e.g., Lentil, Bean Soup, etc.   Stews—Meat, Mince, etc.
    Fish—Baked or Steamed.   Vegetables—Steamed or cooked by conservative method (page 37)
    Eggs, Milk, Butter.   Milk Puddings.   Fruit—Raw or stewed.   Horlicks, Ovaltine, etc.

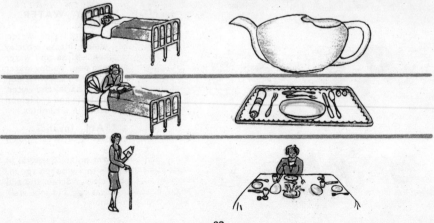

PRESERVES.

INSTRUCTIONS.

Fruit. Should be dry and not too ripe. There is less acid in over-ripe fruit and acid is needed to make jam set.

Sugar. Should be of good quality.

Jars should be free from cracks, clean and warmed before-hand.

Pan. Use a very clean brass or aluminium jam-pan.

Enamelled or thin pans are not suitable.

Make sure that sugar has dissolved before jam boils.

Stir frequently with a wooden spoon.

Boil jam quickly, marmalade slowly.

To Test for Readiness. Put a drop of jam on a saucer. It should "jell" when cool. Remove scum and pour jam into warm jars $\frac{1}{4}$-inch from the top of jar.

Cover at once or leave till cold and cover with waxed circles and jam pot covers. Label with name of jam and date of making.

RASPBERRY JAM.

7 lbs. raspberries.
7 lbs. sugar.

Method.
Warm jam-jars.
Pick over fruit,
put in pan and
heat gently, crush-
ing the berries with a
wooden spoon. Add
sugar when jam is nearly
boiling and stir well.
Boil for 3 minutes. Skim
jam, test and pour into warm
jars, cover and label.

BLACKCURRANT JAM.

Recipe.   8 lbs. currants.   4 pints water.
13 lbs. sugar.

Method. Warm jam-jars. Wash currants, remove stalks and put in jam-pan with water. Bring to the boil and simmer for 10 minutes. Add sugar and boil quickly 20 to 30 minutes. Skim, test and pour into warm jars. Cover and label.

STRAWBERRY JAM.

Recipe.   7 lbs. strawberries.   7 lbs. sugar.
                     Juice of 2 lemons.

Method.   Warm jars.   Husk the berries and put into pan with sugar and lemon Juice.   Heat slowly, stirring till sugar is dissolved.   Bring slowly to the boil, then boil quickly for 15 to 20 minutes or till jam sets.   Test a few drops on a saucer, skim, pour into warm jars, label and store.

RHUBARB JAM.

Recipe.   7 lbs. rhubarb.   7 lbs. sugar.
                     ½ lb. preserved ginger.

Method.   Prepare rhubarb (page 51) and cut in small pieces.   Add chopped ginger and sugar and soak in a basin for 24 hours, covered with a baking-board.   Warm jam-jars.   Stir till boiling then boil quickly for about ½ hour.   Test a few drops on a saucer, skim, pour into warm jars, label and store.

PLUM JAM.

Recipe.   7 lbs. plums.   7 lbs. sugar.
                     ½ to ¾ pint water.

Method.   Heat jars.   Wipe plums.   Put plums and water into pan with low heat and soften slightly before adding sugar.   After adding sugar, stir till sugar dissolves.   Bring to the boil and boil for about 25 minutes.   Skim stones, etc., test, pour and label.

GOOSEBERRY JAM.

Recipe.   2 lbs. gooseberries.   1 teacup water or rhubarb juice.
                     2 lbs. sugar.

Method.   Heat jars.   Top and tail gooseberries, wash and put in jam-pan with water or juice and boil for about 20 minutes till soft.   Add sugar and bring slowly to the boil, stirring occasionally with a wooden spoon.   Boil quickly for 10 minutes.   Test jam, skim, pour into jars, cover and label.

DRIED APRICOT JAM.

Recipe.   2 lbs. dried apricots.   5 pints water.
                     6 lbs. sugar.   2 or 3 lemons.

Method.   Wash the apricots, cut up and soak with the water overnight.   Warm the jars.   Put apricots and water into jam-pan with sugar, grated rind and lemon juice.   Boil up slowly, stirring occasionally with a wooden spoon. Boil quickly for ½ hour till jam sets.   Skim and test. Pour into warm jars, cover and label.

RED CURRANT JELLY.

Method. Wash the currants and put them in a jelly-pan with just enough cold water to cover. Bring to the boil and simmer gently about 20 minutes till currants become pulpy. Strain through jelly-bag. Heat jelly-jars.

Measure juice into pan, bring to the boil and add sugar, allowing 1 lb. sugar to each pint juice. Stir jelly till it boils again and continue boiling 7 to 10 minutes. Test jelly, skim, pour into jars, cover and label.

MARMALADE.

Recipe.
- 2 lbs. bitter oranges.
- 2 lemons.
- 7 lbs. sugar.
- 6 pints water.

Method. Wash fruit, cut off very thin rind and shred it finely. Slice oranges, removing pips. Tie pips in muslin and steep in a little cold water overnight. Pass sliced oranges and rind through mincer and steep with 6 pints water overnight. Heat jam-jars. Put orange pulp and water from pips into jam-pan. Bring to the boil and boil till rind is soft. Add sugar and boil for 30 minutes or till marmalade sets. Pour into warm jars, cover and label.

LEMON CURD.

Recipe.　2 ozs. butter.
　　　　　Rind and juice of two
　　　　　　　　　　　　lemons.
　　　　　3 ozs. sugar.
　　　　　2 eggs.

Method.
Melt butter in
saucepan, wash
lemons, grate rind
then squeeze juice.
Add to butter in pan along
with sugar.
Beat the eggs and add, stirring
well with a wooden spoon. Heat
very slowly. Remove from heat as soon
as the mixture thickens.
Pour into jars, cover and label.

MINCEMEAT.

Recipe.

4 ozs. raisins.	Rind and juice of 1 lemon.
4 ozs. sultanas.	$\frac{1}{2}$ teasp. ground nutmeg.
4 ozs. currants.	$\frac{1}{2}$ teasp. cinnamon.
4 ozs. suet.	$\frac{1}{2}$ teasp. ground ginger.
4 ozs. brown sugar.	$\frac{1}{2}$ teasp. mixed spice.
2 ozs. mixed peel.	$\frac{1}{4}$ teasp. salt.
2 apples.	

Method.
Wash and pick
over raisins, currants
and sultanas, re-
moving stalks.
Split, stone and chop
raisins. Prepare apples
(page 50) and chop finely.
Add chopped suet and chopped
peel. Grate lemon rind and
squeeze juice. Put all ingredients
into mixing bowl. Measure spices,
sugar and salt. Mix all together thoroughly
then press into jars, cover and label.

TOMATO CHUTNEY.

2 lbs. tomatoes.   I lb. onions.
2 lbs. apples.   I oz. salt.
I lb. brown sugar.
$\frac{1}{2}$ oz. ground ginger.
$\frac{1}{2}$ oz. curry powder.
I pint vinegar.

Method.
Warm jars.
Prepare tomatoes
(page 36) and cut in small
pieces. Prepare apples
(page 50) and chop finely.
Skin and chop onion finely
on plate. Put all together in
a lined pan with the vinegar,
sugar, curry powder, salt and
ground ginger and stir well with a
wooden spoon till mixture is soft.
Simmer for $\frac{1}{2}$ hour. Pour into jars, cover
and label.

BOTTLING.

Aim. To create a vacuum so that the germs
cannot thrive.

INSTRUCTIONS.
Fruit should be of an even size and with no
bruises. It should be fresh and not over-ripe.
Bottles. Various types of jars may be used,
e.g., Kilner jars, supplied with rubber bands
and screw-caps or jam jars may be used and
rubber bands, lids and clips may be bought to
fit jars. Jars may also be sealed with hot
mutton fat or wax. Jars should be free from
cracks and lids should fit well.
Rubber rings and lids should be scalded and
left in the water till required.

Pan. A fish kettle is the best (page 11) or a large deep pan. Place a towel or cardboard in the
bottom of the pan.
Preparation of Fruit. Wash and select suitable fruit. Pack tightly into jars, using the handle
of a wooden spoon.
Tomatoes may be used whole, halved or pulped.
Plums. Whole or halved.
Peaches, Pears, etc. Remove skin and halve.
Rhubarb. Wash and cut in inch lengths.

BOTTLED TOMATOES.
(Oven Method)

Tomatoes.	Sugar.
Salt.	Boiling Water.

NOTE. Rhubarb, Plums, Pears, Peaches, Damsons, etc., may be bottled in this way.

Omit sugar and salt. Have boiling syrup ready to fill jars. (page 11).

Method. Pour boiling water over rubber bands and lids and leave in water till required.
Have clips ready. Wash tomatoes. Wash and scald jam-jars by holding for a second over steam from kettle. Measure sugar and salt into saucer, allowing 1 teaspoonful of each to each jar. Pack tomatoes into jars, either whole or halved and sprinkle sugar and salt in layers throughout. Fill jars to top. Place jars on tray, having a space between each jar. Heat oven. Place tray in oven and cover with another tray. Heat very slowly for 1 to 1½ hours. Remove from oven and fill immediately with boiling water till overflowing. Cover quickly with lids, press down clips and leave 24 hours. Remove clips and test.

BOTTLED PLUMS.
Syrup for Bottling.
¼ lb. sugar.
1 pint water.

Method.
Prepare syrup by boiling sugar and water slowly. Boil for 5 minutes, remove scum and leave to cool. Wash plums and pack into jar, using handle of wooden spoon. Pour syrup over till full. Shake jar gently and fill up again if necessary Place on rubber ring (previously prepared) glass lid and metal screw-caps. Give screw ½ turn back. Place a layer of cardboard in bottom of pan. Put jars in but do not allow them to touch each other. Fill with cold water to cover jars and bring very slowly to the boil (1 to 1½ hours). Boil for 7 to 10 minutes. Allow to cool slightly and remove from pan. Screw up tightly. Leave till following day then un-loosen screw and test for a good vacuum.

SWEETS AND CONFECTIONERY.

TREACLE TOFFEE.

Recipe.
1 lb. brown sugar.
4 tablespoons treacle.
1 gill water.
A few drops vinegar.
3 to 4 ozs. butter,
or margarine.

Method.
Grease baking-
tin with lard.
Measure sugar,
treacle, butter
water and vinegar
into a strong metal
pan and stir with a
wooden spoon while
bringing slowly to the
boil. Boil for 10 to 15 mins.
without stirring. (Be careful that toffee does not burn).
Test a few drops in cold water (the
toffee should set and brittle).
Pour into greased tin and leave to
harden. Break into pieces when cold.

VANILLA TABLET.

Recipe.   2 lbs. sugar.
$1\frac{1}{2}$ teacups milk.
1 oz. butter.
Flavouring.

Method.
Grease tin
lightly.
Warm milk and
sugar very slowly
till sugar dissolves.
When boiling add butter.
Boil for 15 minutes then
remove from heat, add
2 teaspoonfuls vanilla essence
and whisk till creamy and
thick.
Pour into tin and mark in squares.
Leave to set.

PEPPERMINT CREAMS.

Recipe. ½ lb. icing sugar.
White of egg.
Essence of peppermint.

Method.
Sieve icing
sugar.
Break egg over
bowl allowing the
white of egg to run into
bowl. Mix icing sugar with
enough white of egg to make
a stiff paste. Add a few drops of
peppermint essence from a teaspoon. Spread board with icing sugar
and roll out paste to ½-inch. Cut out
rounds with small cutter and leave on
grease-proof paper to harden.

MARZIPAN.

Recipe. ½ lb. ground almonds.
¼ lb. icing sugar.
¼ lb. brown sugar.
1 egg.

Method.
Sieve icing
sugar. Add
brown sugar and
ground almonds and
mix well.
Add sufficient egg
to make a stiff paste.
Sprinkle board with
icing sugar and roll out
paste to about 1-inch thick.
If cake is uneven on top remove a thin layer. Brush cake with
egg and lay marzipan to cover exactly.
INSET.

Marzipan Walnuts. Press a walnut on
each side of a small ball of marzipan.
Marzipan Dates. Split date in half, remove
stone and insert a ball of marzipan.

TO ICE A CAKE.

Recipe for Water Icing.

1 lb. icing sugar.
Boiling water
Cochineal.
Vanilla.

Method.

Crush out lumps
in icing sugar with
rolling-pin.
Put sugar in small
bowl and add boiling
water, drop by drop,
very carefully from a teaspoon. Test by coating the
back of wooden spoon. Add
colouring and flavouring.
Have cake on wire tray with
plate underneath to catch drips.
Pour icing on to centre of cake and
spread over top and sides with knife
dipped in boiling water. Arrange walnuts
or other decoration and leave icing to set.

BUTTER ICING.

4 ozs. fresh butter.
6 ozs. icing sugar.
Colouring.
Flavouring.

Method.

Crush icing
sugar till
smooth and
cream well
with fresh butter.
Add flavouring and
colouring from a tea-
spoon and mix.
Insert mixture in icing
bag or syringe. Press
steadily when piping.
NOTE. For beginners it is
a good idea to practice piping
with creamed potato on the lid of a
tin. Icing bag can be made from close-
woven cotton or grease-proof paper.

CREAM SUBSTITUTE.

Recipe. I gill milk.   I oz. butter.
            ½ oz. cornflour.   ½ oz. sugar.
            Pinch salt.   Few drops vanilla.

Method. Blend cornflour and milk in bowl, using a wooden spoon. When smooth and free from lumps, pour into pan and stir till it boils. Cook for 5 minutes. Add salt, stir, and leave aside to cool. Beat butter and sugar together in a bowl till creamy, using a wooden spoon. When cornflour sauce is cold beat it in gradually. Add a few drops of vanilla from a teaspoon, stir and use as required.

ODD DISHES.

BOILED RICE.
(For serving with curry).

Recipe. ¼ lb. patna rice.   Squeeze lemon juice.
            Salt.   Butter.

Method. Measure rice into bowl and wash well under cold water tap. Boil water in pan with salt. Add rice and boil for 12 minutes without a lid, till grains are tender. Drain, then rush cold water through strainer to separate grains. Place rice in buttered paper in pan and place at side of fire to reheat. Cover pan with lid and leave ½ hour. Serve with curry.

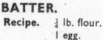

Method. Measure flour into bowl. Break egg into a cup and, if fresh, drop straight into flour. Add salt. Measure milk. Add half the milk and stir till all is well-mixed. Beat for 10 minutes with a wooden spoon to incorporate as much air as possible into the batter. Add rest of milk and stir gently. Remove spoon and cover bowl with a plate. Lay aside for ½ hour to cool before using.

BATTER.

Recipe. ¼ lb. flour.
            1 egg.
            ½ pint milk.
            Pinch salt.

PORRIDGE.

I oz. oatmeal.   ½ pint water.
½ teaspoon salt.

Method. Heat porridge plate. Boil water and salt, stir in oatmeal and continue simmering 20 to 30 minutes, stirring occasionally with a porridge stick. Porridge should look like thick cream when ready. Serve hot, with a jug of cream or milk.

GRUEL.

I oz. oatmeal.   I pint water.
Pinch salt.

Heat plate. Measure oatmeal and water into a bowl, cover and leave to soak for ½ hour. Stir and strain into pan, add salt and stir till it boils. Simmer slowly for 10 minutes. Serve on hot plate with milk.

SAVOURY DUMPLINGS.

Recipe.
1½ to 2 ozs. suet.
4 ozs. flour.
Sprig of parsley.

¼ teaspoonful baking powder.
⅛ teaspoonful salt.

Method. Prepare and chop parsley. Measure flour into bowl. Put half of the measured flour on to board. Remove skin from suet, mix suet with the flour on the board, shred and chop finely. Scrape the suet and flour into the bowl. Measure baking powder and salt and add chopped parsley. Mix well. Add enough cold water to make a fairly stiff consistency, using a knife for mixing. Form into balls, and drop into the stew. Allow 30 to 40 minutes for dumplings to cook. They should be well-risen and very spongy.

BREAD RASPINGS.

Break up pieces of stale bread and spread out in baking-tin. Place tin in very slow oven till breadcrumbs are crisp and golden-brown. Roll out on board, sieve and store in jar or tin.

TOAST.

1 Slice bread. Cut bread thinly, remove crusts and brown slightly under grill or before the fire. Stand upright to cool (cut in dainty fingers if for an invalid). Serve neatly in toast-rack.

TO CLARIFY MARGARINE.

Place margarine in pan and heat very slowly. Remove scum from top. Pour off liquid slowly and use this for greasing tins, pie-dishes, etc. Fluted patty tins can be greased by using a pastry-brush, dipped in clarified margarine.

TO CLEAN FAT.

When fat has become dark in use, turn it into a pan and cover with cold water. Bring slowly to the boil and simmer 15 to 20 minutes. Pour all into a basin of cold water and leave over-night to harden fat. Lift out fat carefully, scrape under side to remove sediment and heat fat slowly to drive off the water. When fat is faintly smoking hot it is ready for use.

TABLE-SETTING.
BREAKFAST TABLE.

REQUIREMENTS.

1. Felt or set of cork mats, tablecloth, 4 table napkins, tea cosy.
2. **Cutlery.** 4 porridge spoons (dessert), 4 dinner forks and knives (large) 4 tea knives (small), serving spoon and fork (large), 4 teaspoons, 1 sugar spoon, 2 butter knives, 1 marmalade spoon.
3. **China.** 4 breakfast cups and saucers, 4 tea plates, 2 butter plates, 1 marmalade dish. Plates with rolls, bread, etc., toast rack.

Teapot and hot water jug in kitchen to heat—also plates for porridge and ashet and plates for egg, etc.

4 COURSE DINNER TABLE FOR 4 PERSONS.

REQUIREMENTS.

1. Table felt or set of cork mats. Serving cloths (2) for table ends, table napkins (4), tablecloth.
2. **Cutlery.** 4 soup spoons (tablespoons), I soup ladle, 4 fish forks and knives, 4 dinner knives and forks (large) 4 dessert spoons and forks (small), 4 tea knives (small) 4 serving spoons (tablespoons).
3. **China and Glass.** 4 side plates (tea plates), 4 tumblers, I water jug, salt and peppers, flowers.

Dishes to be heated in kitchen. 4 soup plates (large), I soup tureen, 4 fish plates, 4 meat plates (large), 4 dessert plates, vegetable dishes, etc.

Before setting the table you must know.

1. What the menu is.
2. How many persons are going to sit down.
3. At what time the meal is going to be served.

COFFEE-TRAY.

AFTERNOON TEA-TABLE.

REQUIREMENTS.

Tray, traycloth, tea-cosy, 3 cups, 3 saucers, 3 teaspoons, sugar basin, cream jug and slop bowl, 2 cork mats (for tea-pot and hot water jug).

Teacloth for table, 3 tea napkins.

Cakestand with plates and d'oyleys, Teapot and hot water jug in kitchen.

INDEX.

INDEX.